DK EYEWITNESS

TOP **10**
BRUSSELS
BRUGES, ANTWERP AND GHENT

Top 10 Brussels, Bruges, Antwerp & Ghent Highlights

The Top 10 of Everything

CONTENTS

Brussels, Bruges, Antwerp & Ghent Area by Area

Streetsmart

Within each Top 10 list in this book, no hierarchy of quality or popularity is implied. All 10 are, in the editor's opinion, of roughly equal merit.

Title page, front cover and spine *The distinctive Atomium towering above Bruparck, Brussels* ***Back cover, clockwise from top left*** *Belgian chocolates; Ghent's canal; Brussels' restaurants; Brussels' Atomium; Bruges' Belfort*

The rapid rate at which the world is changing is constantly keeping the DK Eyewitness team on our toes. While we've worked hard to ensure that this edition of Brussels, Bruges, Antwerp & Ghent is accurate and up-to-date, we know that opening hours alter, standards shift, prices fluctuate, places close and new ones pop up in their stead. So, if you notice we've got something wrong or left something out, we want to hear about it. Please get in touch at **travelguides@dk.com**

Welcome to
Brussels, Bruges, Antwerp & Ghent

Brussels, capital of Europe, and the three great cities of Flanders offer extraordinary riches at every turn. Fabulous art, trend-setting design and fashion, outstanding restaurants, some of the world's best beer and chocolate, and a heritage that has flourished since the 16th century. With this DK Eyewitness Top 10 guide, they're yours to explore.

The splendours of the 16th century are showcased in the paintings of Jan van Eyck, Hans Memling and their contemporaries, housed in such places as the **Musées Royaux des Beaux-Arts** in Brussels and the **Groeningemuseum** in Bruges. This artistic brilliance soared again to new heights with Rubens, whose works can be viewed in the **Koninklijk Museum voor Schone Kunsten (KMSKA)** in Antwerp. The architecture here is just as impressive: visit the medieval **Burg** in Bruges, the Gothic **Antwerp Cathedral** and the splendid Gothic and Flemish Baroque **Grand Place** in Brussels.

Cultural attractions apart, these are also walkable cities, adapted for modern living, with elegant shopping streets, lively cafés, star-spangled restaurants – and the world's best twice-fried *frites*.

Whether you're coming for a weekend or a week, our Top 10 guide explores the best of everything these cities can offer, from the glass trumpets of the **Musée des Instruments de Musique** in Brussels and the cutting-edge contemporary art of the **SMAK** gallery in Ghent, to the enchanting backwaters of Eastern Bruges and the vibrant clubs of Antwerp. There are tips throughout, from seeking out what's free to finding the liveliest festivals, plus easy-to-follow itineraries, designed to tie together a clutch of sights in a short space of time. Add inspiring photography and detailed maps, and you've got the essential pocket-sized travel companion. **Enjoy the book, and enjoy Brussels, Bruges, Antwerp and Ghent**.

Clockwise from top: Lier near Antwerp, Blinde Ezelstraat, Bruges, waffles, Le Botanique, Brussels, Rodin's *The Thinker*, Brussels, Grand Place, Brussels, Comics Art Museum, Brussels

Exploring Brussels, Bruges, Antwerp & Ghent

With so much on offer, these cities are at their best day and night, and there is much to see beyond the main museums and attractions. Part of the pleasure is ambling about the pedestrian-friendly streets and savouring time spent in the restaurants and cafés. These two- and seven-day itineraries will help you make the most of these four fascinating Belgian cities.

Église St-Jean-Baptiste du Béguinage

Place des Martyrs

Comics Art Museum

Place Sainte-Catherine

BRUSSELS

La Bourse

Galeries Royales Saint-Hubert

Grand Place

Cathédrale des Saints Michel et Gudule

Parc tram stop

Parc de Bruxelles Warande

TRAM

0 metres   400
0 yards   400

Musée des Instruments de Musique

Musées Royaux des Beaux-Arts

Horta Museum 2.5 km (1.5 miles)

Key
— Two-day itinerary
— Seven-day itinerary

The Grand Place is dominated by Brussels' magnificent town hall.

Two Days in Brussels

Day ❶
MORNING
Start at the **Grand Place** (see pp14–15). Walk through the **Galeries Royales Saint-Hubert** (see p77) to reach the **Cathédrale des Saints Michel et Gudule** (see p74).
AFTERNOON
After lunch, head to the **Musée des Instruments de Musique** (see pp20–21; closed Mon) and the **Musées Royaux des Beaux-Arts** (see pp18–19; closed Mon).

Day ❷
MORNING
Visit **La Bourse** (see p16), and walk via the Place Sainte-Catherine to the

Musées Royaux des Beaux-Arts is made up of three integrated museums.

Église St-Jean-Baptiste au Béguinage *(see p75)*. Wander through the **Place des Martyrs** *(see p76)* on the way to the **Comics Art Museum** *(see pp26–7; closed Mon, except Jul & Aug)*.
AFTERNOON
Take a tram to the **Horta Museum** *(see pp22–3; closed Mon)*. Wander through the Art Nouveau streets around here.

Seven Days in Brussels, Bruges, Ghent & Antwerp

BRUSSELS – Day ❶
As day one of Two Days in Brussels.

BRUGES – Day ❷
MORNING
Go to the **Markt** and climb the **Belfort** *(see p91)* for a panoramic view. After, head for the **Burg** *(see pp28–9)*.
AFTERNOON
Walk to **Groeningemuseum** *(see pp30–31; closed Mon)*, with its outstanding collection of Flemish masters. Explore the **Onze-Lieve-Vrouwekerk** *(see p92)* and then the **Sint-Janshospitaal** *(see p92; closed Mon)*. Walk on to the **Begijnhof** *(see p93)*.

BRUGES – Day ❸
MORNING
Begin at **Choco-Story** and/or the **Frietmuseum** *(see p94)*, then walk via

the **Sint-Walburgakerk** *(see p94)* into the pleasantly quiet district of **Eastern Bruges** *(see p95)* to visit the **Sint-Annakerk** and the **Volkskundemuseum** *(closed Mon)*.
AFTERNOON
Spend the afternoon at the extraordinary **Jeruzalemkapel** *(closed Sun)* and the neighbouring **Kantcentrum** *(see p95)*, the lace centre, which has demonstrations in the afternoon. Finish by exploring the streets of Eastern Bruges further.

Jeruzalemkapel is a 15th-century hidden gem next to the Kantcentrum.

Key

━━ Seven-day itinerary

Exploring Brussels, Bruges, Antwerp & Ghent

Korenlei, one of Antwerp's attractive quays, is a pick-up point for boat trips.

Seven Days in Brussels, Bruges, Ghent & Antwerp

GHENT – Day ❹

MORNING

Make a pilgrimage to see *The Adoration of the Mystic Lamb (see pp32–3)* in **Sint-Baafskathedraal** *(see p109)*, then ascend the **Belfort tower** *(see p109)*. Continue on to the Sint-Michielsbrug on the **Graslei and Korenlei** *(see p109)* for the views.

AFTERNOON

Take a canal trip, visit **Huis van Alijn** folklore museum *(see p110; closed Mon)*, then wander around the quaint **Patershol** district *(see p54)* behind the museum.

GHENT – Day ❺

MORNING

Take a tram to Ghent's two great art galleries, **MSK** and **SMAK** *(see p111; closed Mon)*.

AFTERNOON

Walk back across the Citadelpark to visit the **STAM** city museum *(see p110; closed Mon)* before returning to the city centre.

Key

— Seven-day itinerary

0 metres 500
0 yards 500

The Adoration of the Mystic Lamb is the star attraction in the Sint-Baafskathedraal in Ghent.

Antwerp Cathedral dominates the medieval market square.

ANTWERP – Day ❻
MORNING
Admire the guildhouses and town hall in the **Grote Markt** (see p101), then walk to **Antwerp Cathedral** (see pp34–5). Visit the **Museum Vleeshuis** (see p102; closed Mon–Wed).
AFTERNOON
Visit the **Sint-Pauluskerk** (see p104), then continue further north to the dockside **Museum Aan de Stroom** (see p102; closed Mon).

ANTWERP – Day ❼
MORNING
To avoid the crowds, get an early start at the **KMSKA** (see pp34–5), then admire the decorative arts of the **Museum Mayer van den Bergh** (see p102; closed Mon).
AFTERNOON
Take in some radical contemporary art at **MUKHA** gallery (see p104; closed Mon), and visit the nearby **FotoMuseum Provincie Antwerpen (FoMu)** (see p104; closed Mon). To finish your trip, head back to the old city centre via the **Museum Plantin-Moretus** (see p102; closed Mon).

FotoMuseum Provincie (FoMu) covers every aspect of photography.

Museum Aan de Stroom

❻

Sint-Pauluskerk

Museum Vleeshuis

ANTWERP

Grote Markt

Antwerp Cathedral

Museum Plantin-Moretus

Museum Mayer van den Bergh

❼

MUKHA

FotoMuseum Provinci Antwerpen

Koninklijk Museum voor Schone Kunsten

| 0 metres | | 600 |
| 0 yards | | 600 |

Key
━ Seven-day itinerary

Top 10 Brussels, Bruges, Antwerp & Ghent Highlights

The magnificent architecture
of the Grand Place, Brussels

TOP 10 Brussels, Bruges, Antwerp & Ghent Highlights

The four great cities of northern Belgium share a rich cultural heritage, yet they are very different. Each, in its own way, is hugely rewarding – not only in cultural sights, but also in delightful and welcoming places to stay, eat and drink.

① The Grand Place

For architectural theatre, the centrepiece of Brussels is hard to beat – as it was three centuries ago (see pp14–15).

② Musées Royaux des Beaux-Arts

Rubens, Van Dyke, Magritte – this splendid collection reveals some of art's greatest names (see pp18–19).

③ Musée des Instruments de Musique

Housed in a magnificent Art Nouveau building, the "mim" contains thousands of instruments (see pp20–21).

④ Horta Museum

Victor Horta was the original Art Nouveau architect; his own house is an expression of this and preserved as a shrine to Art Nouveau (see pp22–3).

Central Brussels

0 metres 500
0 yards 500

2.5 km
(1.5 miles)

⑤ Comics Art Museum

Dedicated to the comic strip, this place reveals all there is to know about this very Belgian art form: Tintin and beyond (see pp26–7).

The Burg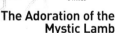

The old centre of Bruges is an architectural gem – a small, intimate square surrounded by historic gabled buildings, each one embellished with fascinating detail *(see pp28–9)*.

Groeningemuseum and Sint-Janshospitaal

Great Flemish artists of the early 15th century were among the first to perfect the technique of oil painting. These two collections demonstrate their extraordinary skills *(see pp30–31)*.

The Adoration of the Mystic Lamb

This multi-panel altarpiece created in 1426–32 by Jan van Eyck and his brother Hubrecht is a great cultural treasure of Europe *(see pp36–7)*.

Koninklijk Museum voor Schone Kunsten (KMSKA)

The Royal Museum of Fine Arts is home to an impressive collection of masterpieces *(see pp34–5)*.

Antwerp Cathedral

Antwerp's cathedral is the city's main landmark, and the largest Gothic church in Belgium. Its impressive interior has some exceptional triptychs *(see pp32–3)*.

🔟 ⭐ The Grand Place

Brussels' Grand Place is the focal point of the city, a tirelessly uplifting masterpiece of unified architecture. Full of symbolic sculpture and gilding, for centuries this was the economic and administrative heart of the city. It was the setting for markets, fairs, pageants and jousts, for the proclamation of decrees, and for public executions. Even without its old political and economic prestige the Grand Place still hums with activity.

⑤ Hôtel de Ville
The Town Hall was the first major building on the Grand Place. Largely rebuilt since its 15th-century beginnings, it still has its original spire, with a statue of St Michael killing the devil.

① Le Cornet
This elaborate building (No 6) was once the guildhouse of the boatmen. Its adornments include a top storey resembling the stern of a ship **(above)**.

② Le Cygne
"The Swan" (No 9) was rebuilt as a private residence in 1698, but in 1720 it was acquired by the Guild of Butchers. It later became a café, and Karl Marx held meetings of the German Workers' Party here.

③ Le Renard
No 7 was a *gildehuis* (guildhouse) – the prestigious headquarters of the Guild of Haberdashers. A gilded statue of a fox **(right)** sits above the door, reflecting the building's old name (Le Renard).

④ Maison des Brasseurs
Called l'Arbre d'Or (the Golden Tree), the brewers' guildhouse (No 10) was designed by Guillaume de Bruyn. It is still used by the Confédération des Brasseurs, and houses a small museum of brewing **(left)**.

NEED TO KNOW
MAP C3

Hôtel de Ville: 02 548 04 47; guided tours start 2pm Wed, 10am, 3pm & 4pm Sun; arrive 15 min before; tour €8

Maison du Roi (Musée de la Ville de Bruxelles): open 10am–5pm Tue–Sun; closed public hols; 02 279 43 50; adm €8

Maison des Brasseurs/Belgian Brewers Museum: open 11am–6pm Wed–Sat; 02 511 49 87; adm €5

■ There are two bar-restaurants here – both pricey, but worth it for their Bruxellois style: Le Roy d'Espagne at No 1 and La Chaloupe d'Or at Nos 24–25. 'T Kelderke at No 15 serves classic Flemish dishes in 7th-century brick-vaulted cellars.

■ A tourist office in the Hôtel de Ville is useful for information.

⑥ Maison du Roi

This medieval-style "King's House" is home to the Musée de la Ville de Bruxelles, a miscellany of city history, including costumes designed for the Manneken-Pis statue *(see p16)*.

⑧ The Tapis de Fleurs

Every even-numbered year for five days in mid-August, the Grand Place is taken over by a massive floral display known as the Carpet of Flowers **(below)**.

NOT QUITE THE REAL THING

The guildhouses of the Grand Place are built largely in the Flemish Renaissance style of the late 16th and early 17th centuries. Little of it actually dates from this period, however. On 13–14 August 1695, under the orders of Louis XIV, French troops led by Marshal de Villeroy lined up their cannons, took aim at the spire of the Hôtel de Ville, and pulverized the city centre. In defiance, the citizens set about reconstructing the Grand Place, a task that was completed in just five years.

Map of the Grand Place

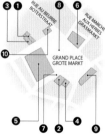

⑦ Statue of Everard 't Serclaes

Famous Brussels resident Everard 't Serclaes died here in 1388 resisting Flemish occupation. Superstitious passers-by stroke his bronze statue **(below)** for luck.

⑨ Maison des Ducs de Brabant

The impressive 17th-century façade at the southeast end of the square spans seven houses and is adorned with the busts of the Dukes of Brabant.

⑩ Maison des Boulangers

The bakers' guildhouse at No 1 is coated with symbols, including six figures representing the essential elements of breadmaking. The unusual octagonal lantern on the roof is topped by a striking gilded statue of Fame.

Around the Grand Place

Restaurants line Rue des Bouchers

 Rue des Bouchers
MAP C3

Many of the streets around the Grand Place reflect the trades that once operated there. The "Street of the Butchers" and its intersecting Petite Rue des Bouchers are famous for their lively restaurants and colourful displays of food.

 Musée du Costume et de la Dentelle
MAP C3 ▪ Rue de la Violette 12 ▪ 02 213 44 50 ▪ Open 10am–5pm Tue–Sun ▪ Adm (free first Sun of month)

This small but rewarding museum dedicated to historic costume and lace has a limited but choice selection of exhibits.

 La Bourse
MAP B3 ▪ Bruxella 1238 ▪ 02 279 43 50

Brussels' Stock Exchange, La Bourse is an unmissable feature of the city's landscape, built in 1873 in the style of a Greek temple and lavishly decorated. Following renovations, from 2023 onwards it will also house the "Belgian Beer World", an interactive beer museum, as well as a skybar,

Detail on the façade of La Bourse

restaurant and brasserie. Also here is Bruxella 1238, which displays archaeological finds and the exposed ruins of the Franciscan convent on which La Bourse was built.

 Manneken-Pis
MAP B3 ▪ Corner of Rue de l'Étuve and Rue du Chêne

No one knows why this bronze statue of a boy peeing water has become such a symbol of Brussels. Since the early 18th century, costumes of all kinds have been made for him.

Galeries Royales Saint-Hubert

 Galeries Royales Saint-Hubert
MAP C3

Opened in 1847, this was the first shopping arcade in Europe. It features magnificent vaulted glass ceilings.

 Place Saint-Géry
MAP B3

The square that marks the site of Brussels' first settlement is today dominated by Les Halles de Saint-Géry, an attractive iron and red-brick structure built in 1881 as a meat market. Now a craft market, exhibition space and café, it is the central focus of an area known for its nightlife.

7 Maison Dandoy
MAP C3 ▪ Rue au Beurre 31

Brussels´ best makers of biscuits have been perfecting their craft since 1829. Behind a ravishing shop window lie goodies such as *speculoos*, *sablés* and waffles.

8 Statue of Charles Buls
MAP C3

In Place Agora is one of Brussels' most delightful statues: a portrait of the bearded and moustachioed artist, scholar and reformer Charles Buls (1837–1914) and his dog. Buls, who served as the mayor or Burgomaster from 1891 to 1899, is credited with restoring the Grand Place.

9 Église Saint-Nicolas
MAP C3 ▪ Rue au Beurre 1
▪ 02 213 00 65 ▪ Open 10am–6pm Mon–Fri, 9am–6pm Sat & Sun

St Nicholas of Myra – aka Santa Claus – was patron saint of merchants, and this church has served the traders of the Grand Place since the 14th century. It retains a fine medieval atmosphere, despite desecration by Protestant rebels in the 16th century and damage during the bombardment of 1695.

Église Notre-Dame de Bon Secours

10 Église Notre-Dame de Bon Secours
MAP B3 ▪ Rue du Marché au Charbon 91 ▪ 02 514 31 13
▪ Open 9am–5pm daily

The most striking feature of this delightful church, built between 1664 and 1694, is its soaring hexagonal choir, rising to a domed ceiling. The façade bears the coat of arms of the enlightened 18th-century governor of the Austrian Netherlands, Charles of Lorraine.

THE ÎLE SAINT-GÉRY AND THE RIVER SENNE

Brussels began as a group of little islands on a marshy river. Legend has it that in the 6th century AD, St Géry, Bishop of Cambrai, founded a church here, and a settlement grew around it. The name Broeksele (later Brussels), meaning "house in the swamp", is first mentioned in 966, and a castle was built on the island by Charles, Duke of Lorraine, a decade later, effectively launching the city. The river, called the Senne, ran through the city until the 19th century. Never large, it became overwhelmed by the growing population, and such a health hazard that it was covered over between 1867 and 1871. This process created Boulevard Anspach and Boulevard Adolphe Max, among others, while the river formed part of the city´s new sewer and drainage system. It can still be glimpsed here and there in the city.

The River Senne in 1587

TOP 10 ⭐ Musées Royaux des Beaux-Arts

Brussels' "Royal Museums of the Fine Arts" are a *tour de force.* Many of the great names in art history are represented here. The galleries are divided into three integrated parts: the Old Masters Museum (15th to 18th centuries), the Fin-de-Siècle Museum (19th and early 20th centuries) and the Magritte Museum. Overall, they represent one of the greatest and most comprehensive collections of art from the Low Countries anywhere in the world.

1 Realism to Post-Impressionism (Fin-de-Siècle Museum)

Belgian artists echoed French art movements, but applied their own originality. Social Realism emanates from works by Hippolyte Boulenger; Émile Claus's bucolic scenes reflect the late-Impressionist style of Luminism; Henri Evenepoel's Post-Impressionist style is redolent of Degas; James Ensor prefigured the Expressionists **(right)**.

2 Early Netherlandish Painting (Old Masters Museum)

The museum's collection includes works by Rogier van der Weyden **(above)**, Hans Memling, Dirk Bouts, Petrus Christus, Rachel Ruysch and many others. The "Flemish Primitives" perfected the technique of oil painting, and had a major influence on Italian art.

3 Gillion Crowet Collection (Fin-de-Siècle Museum)

This outstanding collection showcases the work of Art Nouveau masters such as Victor Horta, Émile Gallé, Alphonse Mucha and Fernand Khnopff **(below)**.

4 Old Masters Museum

This rich collection spans the 15th to the 18th centuries, and includes the Flemish Primitives, the 16th-century Master, Pieter Bruegel the Elder, and exquisite works by Rubens, Van Dyck and Jordaens. It focuses on Belgian art and also has work by major European painters such as Claude Lorrain, Tiepolo and Jacques-Louis David (including his *Death of Marat*).

⑤ Magritte Museum

René Magritte's work **(above)** is so often seen in reproduction that it is a treat to see it up close. The museum, in a separate part of the Musées Royaux des Beaux-Arts, houses the world's largest collection of his work.

⑥ Fin-de-Siècle Museum

This museum embraces not just painting and sculpture, but early Art Nouveau artifacts and architecture from 1884 to 1914.

⑦ The Modern Collection

The museum's collection of 20th- and 21st-century art **(below)** is due to move to the Vanderborght building in 2024. Until then, some items are on show in temporary exhibitions.

⑧ The Rubens Collection (Old Masters Museum)

To those who think of Rubens only in terms of scenes filled with plump, naked ladies, this collection comes as a revelation, displaying vigour, spontaneity and artistic risk-taking.

⑨ The Buildings

Set on the crest of the Coudenberg, the old royal enclave of Brussels, the museum's main buildings were designed by one of the leading architects of the day, Belgian Alphonse Balat (1818–95).

⑩ Belgian Symbolism (Fin-de-Siècle Museum)

Look out for the inventiveness and skill of such artists as Léon Spilliaert, Jean Delville and Léon Frédéric.

NEED TO KNOW

MAP C4 ■ Rue de la Régence 3 ■ 02 508 32 11 ■ www.fine-arts-museum.be

Open 10am–5pm Tue–Fri, 11am–6pm Sat–Sun

Adm €15 incl. Old Masters, Fin-de-Siecle, Magritte Museums; €10 incl. Old Masters, Magritte Museums; €10 Magritte Museum; reduced rates for over-65s (€10, €8 & €8); under 19s free & on first Wed of each month after 1pm

■ Each museum has its own cafeteria, but far more exciting is the mim restaurant on top of the nearby Musée des Instruments de Musique *(see pp20–21)*. Also, just a short walk away, are the cafés of the Place du Grand Sablon, including the exquisite *chocolatier* Wittamer *(see p78)*.

■ The museums tend to be quieter mid-week during the middle of the day, so this can be the ideal time for a visit.

Gallery Guide

The Old Masters Museum is set out in sequence on a single, extensive upper floor of the building. The Fin-de-Siècle Museum occupies a spiralling sunken building originally built to house the modern art collection. The Magritte Museum is on five floors in an adjacent building. Visitors can choose to visit each of these individually, but it is far cheaper to buy a "combi" ticket, which permits entry to all.

🔟⭐ Musée des Instruments de Musique

The Musée des Instruments de Musique, often referred to as "Le mim", exhibits musical instruments from ancient to modern, including the largest collection of instruments by Adolphe Sax. The exhibits – selected from a collection totalling more than 7,000 pieces – are beautifully arranged, and headphones permit visitors to hear what the instruments actually sound like. The museum is housed in an exhilarating location: the classic Art Nouveau department store called "Old England".

1 The "Old England" Building

Completed in 1899, this is a classic example of the innovative iron-and-glass structures produced by Art Nouveau architects (below).The interior is equally impressive.

3 Stringed Instruments

Sharing the 2nd floor is the stringed instrument section, including violins (right), psalteries, dulcimers, harps, lutes and guitars, plus a recon-struction of a violin workshop.

4 20th-Century Instruments

Technology has had a major impact on music in the late 20th century, from electric amplifica-tion to synthesizers and computer-generated music. This small collec-tion offers a fascinating snapshot. If you don't know what an *ondes martenot* is, here's your chance to find out.

6 Mechanical Instruments

The ingenuity of instrument-makers is most evident in this collection, which includes some outra-geously elaborate musical boxes and a *carillon* – a set of bells used to play tunes.

5 Non-European Instruments

The mim runs a strong line in ethnomusicology. This impressive collection includes panpipes, sitars, African harps and drums, gamelan orchestras and giant decorative horns (below).

2 The Historical Survey

This section charts the evolution of western "art" instruments from antiquity through the Renaissance to the 19th century. The headphone guide shows the evolving complexity of musical sound.

7 mim Restaurant
Even though the restaurant is currently undergoing renovation, it is worth taking the lift up to the 10th floor to admire the view. From here you can see the statue of St Michael on top of the Hôtel de Ville, and across town to the Basilique Nationale and the Atomium.

Trombone with six valves

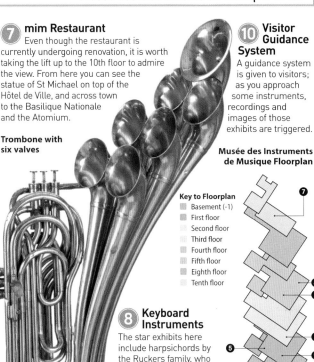

10 Visitor Guidance System
A guidance system is given to visitors; as you approach some instruments, recordings and images of those exhibits are triggered.

Musée des Instruments de Musique Floorplan

Key to Floorplan
- Basement (-1)
- First floor
- Second floor
- Third floor
- Fourth floor
- Fifth floor
- Eighth floor
- Tenth floor

8 Keyboard Instruments
The star exhibits here include harpsichords by the Ruckers family, who worked in Antwerp from the 16th century.

9 European Folk Instruments
This fascinating collection includes pipes, rattles, accordions, hurdy-gurdies and some splendid oddities – chief among them a collection of Belgian glass trumpets.

NEED TO KNOW

MAP D4 ▪ Rue Montagne de la Cour 2 ▪ 02 545 01 30 ▪ www.mim.be

Open 9:30am–5pm Tue–Fri, 10am–5pm Sat & Sun

Adm €8 (under 18s free & on first Wed of every month after 1pm)

▪ Until the restaurant on the top floor reopens, head for the numerous cafés of the Place du Grand Sablon, just a short walk away.

▪ Expect to spend at least two hours in this museum; to do it full justice give it three to four hours. Though the museum closes at 5pm, staff like to empty the exhibition rooms by 4:45pm.

Museum Guide
The museum is set out on four of the building's ten floors. Floor –1 is called "Musicus mechanicus" and features mechanical, electrical and electronic instruments. The 1st floor covers instruments of the world. The 2nd floor is a historical survey of western instruments, from Egyptian origins to 19th-century innovations. The 4th floor is mainly devoted to the history of keyboard and stringed instruments. There is a shop on the 3rd floor, library on the 5th, and a concert hall on the 8th; the restaurant is on the top floor.

🔟 ⭐ Horta Museum

In the late 19th century, Brussels was a centre for avant-garde design, and a rapidly growing city. To feed the market for stylish mansions, architects scavenged history for ideas; the result was the so-called "eclectic style". In 1893, architect Victor Horta created a new style – later labelled "Art Nouveau" – full of free-flowing, naturalistic lines, elaborated with wrought iron, stained glass, mosaics, murals and finely crafted woodwork. Horta brought this style to full maturity when he built his house – now this museum.

1 The Building
When designing for his clients, Horta liked to tailor the house to how they lived. His own house **(right)** has two distinct parts: on the left his residence; on the right, his offices and studio.

2 Furniture
Horta also liked to design the furniture to go in his houses. Although it bears an Art Nouveau stamp, Horta's furniture tends to be simple, restrained and practical.

3 Woodwork
There is a note of austerity as well as luxury in Art Nouveau design. The richly carved wood in the dining room is left natural, allowing the quality of the wood to speak for itself.

6 Scale Model of the Maison du Peuple
Horta was well-known for his designs for commercial and public buildings. The Maison du Peuple was an innovative cast-iron structure built for the Société Coopérative in 1895. A scale model of it can be seen in the cellar.

4 Art Nouveau Sculpture Collection
Throughout the museum are fine sculptures by late 19th-century Belgian artists. Look out for *La Ronde des Heures* **(below)**, in the rear salon on the first floor. This intriguing little bronze was created by Philippe Wolfers (1858–1929), a leading Art Nouveau jeweller and silversmith who worked with Horta.

5 Structural Ironwork
In what was considered a bold gesture at the time, Horta used iron structures to support his houses. He even made a virtue of it, by leaving some of the iron exposed and drawing attention to it with wrought-iron embellishments **(left)**.

7 Leaded Glass
The use of stained glass – shapes of coloured glass held together by lead strips – was embraced by Art Nouveau architects. Examples appear at various points in the house – notably in the door panels and stairwell skylight.

8 Mosaics

The sinuous lines of Art Nouveau design in the mosaic tiling of the dining room floor **(left)** help to soften the effect of the white-enamelled industrial brick lining that covers the walls.

9 The Staircase

The interior design hangs on a central stairwell, lit from the top by a large, curving skylight. The ironwork bannisters **(above)** have been given a typically exuberant flourish.

Fixtures and Fittings 10

Horta was an *ensemblier*: he liked to design an entire building in all its detail, down to the last light fixture **(right)**, door handle and coat hook. This attention to detail conveys the impression of complete architectural mastery: nothing is left to chance.

VICTOR HORTA

The son of a Ghent shoemaker, Victor Horta (1861–1947) studied architecture from the age of 13. After designing the Hôtel Tassel *(see p48)* between 1893 and 1895, his reputation soared. Thereafter he designed houses, department stores and public buildings. With World War I, Art Nouveau fell from favour, and Horta turned to a harder style, seen in his Palais des Beaux-Arts in Brussels. He was awarded the title of Baron in 1932.

NEED TO KNOW

MAP C8 ■ Rue Américaine 27, 1060 BRU (Saint-Gilles)
■ 02 543 04 90
■ www.hortamuseum.be

Open 2–5:30pm Tue–Fri, 11am–5:30pm Sat & Sun; closed public hols; booking ahead is essential

Adm €12; free on first Sun of the month

■ There are several bars and cafés around Place du Châtelain. For a spot of lunch before the museum's 2pm opening hour, try the charming La Canne en Ville *(see p87)* or La Quincaillerie *(see p87)*, dating from 1903, which has plenty of Art Nouveau flair.

■ The Horta Museum is at the heart of a cluster of Art Nouveau buildings. Key streets include Rue Defacqz, Rue Faider and Rue Paul-Émile Janson. Hôtel Hannon is also close by *(see pp48–9)*.

Following pages Cathédrale des Saints Michel et Gudule, Brussels

🔟 ⭐ Comics Art Museum

Tintin is perhaps the most famous Belgian in the world. But this comic-strip hero is just one of hundreds produced in Belgium over the last century. The comic strip – *bande dessinée* in French – is called the "ninth art". The library at Brussels' Comics Art Museum contains 40,000 volumes. Set out in a renovated fabric warehouse, the museum (formerly called the Centre Belge de la Bande Dessinée) presents the history of the form, shows how strips are made, and explores some of the key characters and their creators.

1 Invention of the Comic Strip

This exhibition explores how the comic strip began **(below)**. Discover the history of the art form and its use by civilizations throughout the world – from early cave art to 19th-century magazines.

4 The Building

The museum **(right)** occupies what was formerly the Magasins Waucquez, an Art Nouveau structure of cast iron supporting large expanses of glass, designed by Victor Horta between 1903 and 1906 *(see p49)*.

2 The Art of the Comic Strip

This exhibition contains a selection of original drawings showing how comic strips are made. A wide range of artists, from the traditional to the modern, donated their sketches and studies to demonstrate each step involved in the process of creating a comic strip.

3 Pieter De Poortere Auditorium

Created by Pieter De Poortere, Dickie is a magazine character adopted by the screen. Here you can view comic strip gags and successful cartoons.

5 Slumberland Bookshop

Named after the Little Nemo adventure, the shop stocks everything on the comic strip theme.

6 The Peyo Exhibition

This permanent exhibition is devoted to Peyo, creator of *The Smurfs*. There is a Smurf playhouse that welcomes all visitors.

Comics Art Museum Floorplan

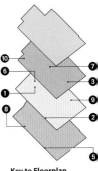

Key to Floorplan
- Ground floor
- First floor
- Second floor
- Third floor

7 Horta and the Waucquez Warehouse

The exhibition covers the fascinating history of this Art Nouveau former warehouse **(left)**.

8 Library

The library has a public reading room, which is open to anyone with a museum ticket.

TINTIN

The story of Tintin goes back to 1929, when he first appeared in a children's newspaper supplement *Le Petit Vingtième*. Brussels-born inventor Hergé (Georges Rémi, *see p42*) created the character as he took him through a series of adventures related to real events, such as the rise of fascism (*King Ottakar's Sceptre*). The charm of Tintin is his naive determination, as well as the multitude of archetypal characters that surround him, such as Captain Haddock and his faithful dog Snowy.

9 The Gallery

The Gallery exhibition space displays a wide range of international albums, both classical as well as contemporary in style. The space is dedicated to new comics from different genres, such as fantasy, satire and crime.

10 Tintin

Of course, the main hero of the museum is the famous boy-reporter Tintin, creation of Hergé. Translated into some 40 languages, over 140 million copies of the books have been sold worldwide. The museum acknowledges his status with displays on key characters **(below)**, and the rocket that went to the moon.

NEED TO KNOW

MAP D2 ■ Rue des Sables 20 ■ 02 219 19 80 ■ www.comicscenter.net

Open 10am–6pm Tue–Sun (Jul–Aug: daily)

Adm €12

■ The museum's own Brasserie Horta serves a good range of lunch dishes. If that doesn't appeal, you are only a 10- to 15-minute walk from the Grand Place and its multitude of cafés and restaurants. Nearer at hand is the bar À la Mort Subite (*see p78*), a traditional place to sample *gueuze* beer.

■ This museum is *not* guaranteed to entertain children, especially if they do not speak French or Dutch. It is, rather, a museum showing the evolution of the craft. Free guides in English.

TOP 10 ⭐ The Burg

Bruges began life in the 10th century as a castle built on marshland formed by the River Reie. The castle has disappeared, but the charming square that replaced it, the Burg, has remained the historic heart of the city. The most impressive building is the Stadhuis, a classic late-medieval town hall built when Bruges was a hub of international trade. Architectural styles from the Gothic Era onwards can be seen in the buildings on the Burg, which disclose fascinating secrets that lie behind this city.

Map of the Burg

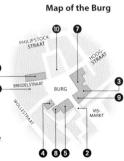

1 Breidelstraat

The quaint little street that connects Bruges' main market place, the Markt, to the Burg is lined with shops selling souvenirs as well as one of the city's most famous products, lace.

2 Blinde Ezelstraat

A lovely street leads off the south of the Burg, beneath the arch **(above)** that links the Oude Griffie to the Stadhuis. The name "Blind Donkey Street" may relate to a nearby inn.

4 Heilig Bloedbasiliek

On the west side of the Burg is the Basilica of the Holy Blood **(right)**, a chapel lavishly restored in Neo-Gothic style in the late 19th century. Its museum holds a relic of blood said to be Christ's.

3 Renaissancezaal van het Brugse Vrije

In the corner of the Burg is the Renaissance Room, whose star exhibit is the Charles V chimneypiece, a virtuoso piece of 16th-century wood carving.

5 Stadhuis
One of medieval Europe's great secular buildings, the Stadhuis (city hall) **(above)** is an expression of Bruges' self-confidence in medieval times. It was built between 1376 and 1421 in the Flamboyant Gothic style.

A bird's-eye view of the Stadhuis and the Burg

6 Proosdij
The Provost's House lining the north side of the Burg is in Flemish Baroque style (1622), with a roof-line balustrade topped by the figure of Justice.

7 Landhuis van het Brugse Vrije
This 18th-century mansion was the headquarters of the "Liberty of Bruges", an administrative jurisdiction covering a large region around the city, while Bruges governed itself separately.

8 St Basil's Chapel
Beneath the Heilig Bloedbasiliek is another chapel of an utterly contrasting mood. Constructed of hefty grey stone in the 12th century, it is a superb and atmospheric example of muscular Romanesque style, and also a reminder of the Burg's origins as a castle.

9 Oude Civiele Griffie
The Renaissance touched Bruges' architecture only lightly; this "Old Civil Registry" is the exception to the rule.

10 The North Side
The little park occupies the site of the Sint-Donaaskerk (see panel). The bronze statue of The Lovers (1986) is by local sculptor Stefaan Depuydt and his wife, Livia Canestraro.

THE MISSING CATHEDRAL

Images of the centre of Bruges before 1799 capture the north side of the Burg occupied by the impressive hulk of the Sint-Donaaskerk. The first church on this site dated back to Bruges' origins, and Jan van Eyck was buried here. Enlarged over the centuries, in 1559 it became the city's cathedral. During the occupation by French revolutionary forces, it was torn down. Parts of its foundations can still be seen in the Crowne Plaza Hotel (see p127).

NEED TO KNOW

MAP L4

Renaissancezaal van het Brugse Vrije: Burg 11a; open 9:30am–5pm daily; adm €7 (under 12s free), included in ticket for Stadhuis

Heilig Bloedbasiliek/ St Basil's Chapel: Burg 13; open 10am–5:15pm daily; the relic can be venerated between 2–4pm daily; adm to Schatkamer (museum): €3 (under 12s free)

Stadhuis: Burg 12; open 9:30am–5pm daily; adm €7 (incl. audio-guide and entrance to Renaissancezaal; under 12s free)

■ De Garre (see p97), just off the Burg, is an ancient café serving drinks and snacks.

■ All the sights in the Burg can been seen in an hour or two.

🔟 ⭐ Two Museums of Bruges

These museums, on separate sites a short distance apart, contain some of the world's finest examples of late medieval art, presenting a selection of work by artists such as Jan van Eyck (c.1390–1441). The Groeningemuseum is a small and charming gallery with a radical edge. The Sint-Janshospitaal, part of the medieval hospital, is devoted to that historic tradition, with the paintings of Hans Memling that were commissioned for its chapel.

1 The Legend of St Ursula

This series of panels by the anonymous "Master of the Saint Ursula Legend" tells the medieval tale of St Ursula and her company of 11,000 virgins, cruelly martyred in pagan Germany **(left)**.

4 The Last Judgment

Hieronymus Bosch (c. 1450–1516) is famous for his paintings of spiritual anguish, torture and hell. This piece in the Groeningemuseum is an insight into the religious psyche of the times.

2 The St Ursula Shrine

Completed by Memling for the Sint-Janshospitaal in 1489, this impressive reliquary **(below)** depicts the Legend of St Ursula in six panels.

NEED TO KNOW

Groeningemuseum:
MAP L4 ■ Dijver 12
■ 050 44 87 11

Open 9:30am–5pm
Tue–Sun; adm €14
(under 12s free)

Sint-Janshospitaal:
MAP K5 ■ Mariastraat 38

Open 9:30am–5pm
Tue–Sun; adm €12 (under
12s free), incl. entry to
Arentshuis *(see p92)*

■ The Groeninge-
museum is only a short
walk from the centre
of town, where there
is a wide choice of cafés
as well as restaurants
(see p97).

■ Available from the
tourist office, the Musea
Brugge card is valid for
three days and gives
access to 13 of Bruges's
top museums (including
the two described here).

The Adoration of the Magi 3

This work, displayed in the Sint-Janshospitaal's chapel, was painted by Memling in 1479. It is known as the Triptych of Jan Floreins after the patron, seen behind a low wall on the left of the central panel **(right)**.

5 The Moreel Triptych

Burgomaster of Bruges, Willem Moreel, commissioned this work from Memling in 1484. Moreel is depicted in the left-hand panel and his wife in the right, with various saints in the middle.

8 Secret-Reflet

This Symbolist work of 1902 by Belgian painter Fernand Khnopff (1858–1921) includes an image of the Sint-Janshospitaal. The title refers to the play on the word "reflection" in the two images.

THE RISE OF BRUGES

Under the dukes of Burgundy Bruges prospered, and in 1419 it became the capital of the Burgundian empire (see p40). The city's elite became wealthy, educated patrons of the arts. The dukes of Burgundy married into European royalty: Philip the Good married Isabella of Portugal; Charles the Bold, Margaret of York. Their marriages were celebrated with vast feasts – the stuff of European legends. This is the world glimpsed in the paintings of the Flemish masters.

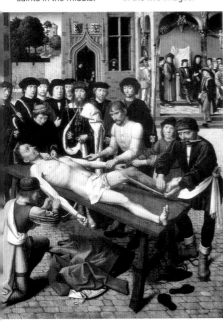

9 Martyrdom of Saint Hippolytus

This 15th-century triptych by Dirk Bouts and Hugo van de Goes, in one scene depicts the saint being pulled apart by four horses – at once horribly gruesome, strangely calm and exquisitely detailed.

10 Madonna with Canon Joris van der Paele

The supreme masterpiece (below) of the Groeningemuseum collection was painted in 1436 by Jan van Eyck. The detail is astonishing.

6 The Judgement of Cambyses

In 1488, Bruges imprisoned their ruler, the Holy Roman Emperor Maximilian. This large diptych (above) by Gerard David depicting the gruesome flaying of a corrupt judge was commissioned for the town hall as a public apology.

7 The Triptych with St John the Baptist and St John the Evangelist

Painted by Memling in 1479, this work celebrates the two St Johns, patron saints and protectors of the Sint-Janshospitaal.

🔟 ⭐ Antwerp Cathedral

Antwerp Cathedral (Onze-Lieve-Vrouwekathedraal) is the largest Gothic church in the Low Countries. Its wedding-cake spire, rising up from a medieval market square, is a major landmark in the city. The cathedral took 170 years to build, and even then was not complete. It was the church of the wealthy guilds, richly adorned with their shrines, reliquaries and altarpieces. Gutted by fire and vandals in the 16th and 18th centuries, the cathedral still has major treasures, notably two triptychs by Rubens.

1 The Raising of the Cross
This triptych, and the impressive *Descent from the Cross* on the other side of the nave, secured Rubens' reputation in Antwerp. The central and right-hand panels display the dynamic energy that was Rubens' hallmark **(below)**.

2 Original Murals
The cathedral was once bright with murals that have fallen away or been overpainted. Restoration has revealed some of these originals.

3 The Pulpit
Elaborately carved oak pulpits feature in many Belgian churches. The subject of this one, the propagation of the faith in the "four" continents, is tackled with extraordinary ambition – a riot of birds, trees, textile swags, angels, saints and symbolic figures.

4 The Nave
The interior **(above)** is bright and uplifting, largely by virtue of its scale, the expanse of glass, and the soaring space that rises to the rib vaults. Unusually, the columns of the aisle have no capitals, so bend seamlessly to form Gothic arches, creating a serene effect.

5 The Burgundian Window
A fair number of the cathedral's original stained-glass windows have survived. The Burgundian is the oldest window, dating from 1503 **(left)**. It depicts Philip the Handsome, the Duke of Burgundy, and his wife Joanna of Castile, with their patron saints behind them.

The Spire ⑥

The cathedral's dainty spire **(right)** was built over about 100 years from the mid-1400s onwards. As it rises to its pinnacle at 123 m (404 ft), it shows increasingly daring Gothic style. The only other comparable spire is that of the Hôtel de Ville in Brussels.

The Cupola ⑨

From outside, the dome looks like a tiered black onion. Inside, its logic is clear: the glass tiers let in light to illuminate the *Assumption of the Virgin* (1647), Cornelis Schut's notable ceiling painting. The effect is of looking straight up into the heavens.

⑩ The Virgin Exalted through Art

The cathedral underwent restoration in the late 19th century. The effort to recreate a medieval effect in some of the chapels behind the choir is admirable. Albrecht De Vriendt's fine triptych shows the "Eyckian" revival at its best.

Cathedral Floorplan

The Madonna ⑦ of Antwerp

This exceptional wooden statue **(above)** has been a focus of devotion since the 16th century, and has a changing wardrobe of robes and crowns.

The Schyven ⑧ Organ

This impressive instrument is housed in a superb 17th-century case created by three leading sculptors of the day.

ICONOCLASTS AND FRENCH REVOLUTIONARIES

Antwerp Cathedral was once richly decorated; two episodes have rendered it rather more austere. The first, during the 1560s, was the onslaught of Protestant zealots, or "iconoclasts", who set about ridding churches of statues, paintings and relics. The second occurred in the 1790s, when the forces of the French Revolution went about demolishing churches, or putting them to secular use as stables, barracks, law courts and factories.

NEED TO KNOW

MAP T2 ■ Groenplatz
■ 03 213 99 51 ■ www.dekathedraal.be

Open 10am–5pm Mon–Fri, 10am–3pm Sat, 1–5pm Sun & public hols

Adm €8, students and over 60s €6, under 18s free

■ There are many cafés, bars and restaurants in the streets around the cathedral. The aptly named Het Elfde Gebod (The Eleventh Commandment) *(see p107)* in Torfbrug has a terrace and an interior decorated with statues of saints and religious artifacts. It serves hearty local fare and an extensive choice of beers.

■ Listen out for the 49 carillon bells that play tunes on the hour. In the summer, carillon concerts are given, when the bells are played from a keyboard.

TOP 10 ⭐ Koninklijk Museum voor Schone Kunsten (KMSKA)

Set within a grandiose historic building, the Royal Museum of Fine Arts contains 8,400 remarkable masterpieces produced by artists from southern Netherlands. The permanent collection, spanning the 14th to the 20th centuries, displays works from the Flemish Primitives through to the modern masters. Closed for over a decade, the museum reopened in 2022, following a €100 million facelift and extensive construction, with 50 state-of-the-art viewing rooms – a homogenous blend of traditional and modern reflecting the artworks within.

4 Museum Garden

Styled in a traditional manner to reflect the long-drawn history and origins of the KMSKA, the museum garden provides a welcome oasis of green in the city (accessible only during museum's opening hours). It also doubles as an open-air gallery.

1 Sculptures on the Façade

Adorning the museum's façade **(above)** are busts of famous artists including Rubens, Michelangelo and Rembrandt, along with four female statues representing architecture, painting, drawing and sculpture. The crowning glory is Thomas Vinçotte's *Triumph of the Fine Arts* (1905).

2 The Rik Wouters Collection

Look out for colourful paintings, intricate drawings and expressive sculptures by Rick Wouters (1882–1916). KMSKA houses the world's largest collection of his artworks. Highlights include Wouters' paintings of scenes from daily life.

5 The Rubens Room

The museum's numerous canvases by Peter Paul Rubens (1577–1640), the master of Flemish Baroque, demonstrate his skill in different disciplines, from religious and mythological works through to portraiture. Don't miss *The Adoration of the Magi*.

3 Madonna Surrounded by Seraphim and Cherubim, 1450

This modern-looking painting **(left)** is a highlight of the museum's collection. Created by the French court painter Jean Fouquet in the mid-15th century, it portrays the Virgin Mary as the Queen of Heaven.

6 The Last Day, 1964

Belgian Expressionist artist, and former member of the CoBra group, Pierre Alechinsky (b. 1927) once stated, "When I paint, I liberate monsters". His painting *The Last Day* is one of the most iconic works on display at KMSKA.

(7) "Welcome" Mosaic

The 76-sq-m (818-sq-ft) mosaic **(below)** at the museum's entrance by Belgian artist Marie Zolamian (b. 1975) is the country's largest such piece of art. It comprises 60 different types of marble and 480,000 tiles in total.

(8) The Van Dyck Room

With gold decorations on the mouldings, beautifully restored stuccowork and cosy parquet flooring, this stately gallery – one of the museum's original rooms – displays masterpieces by Van Dyck (1599–1641).

BEHIND THE SCENES

KMSKA is an internationally renowned research institution, with its own conservation studio. It is also the only Flemish museum with special scientific status for analysing artworks, and learning about techniques, colours and materials. The museum's "Artists in Residence" programme embraces musicians, dancers, poets, actors and playwrights as well as artists and sculptors, providing a rich environment to nurture new talent.

(9) The Vegetable Market, 1567

Antwerp artist Joachim Beuckelaer – famed for painting market scenes such as *The Vegetable Market* – was influential in the development of still life art across Renaissance Europe.

(10) The Ensor Collection

The world's largest collection of works by Belgium Modernist James Ensor (1860–1949) are on display in the modern wing of the museum. Masks feature prominently, as do still lifes **(below)**, skeletons and seascapes.

NEED TO KNOW

MAP S3 ■ Leopold de Waelplaats
■ 03 224 95 50 ■ www.kmska.be

■ Grab a bite at the café and coffee bar on-site. Alternatively, head to Murni Zuid *(Leopold de Waelplaats 10)* across the museum. The nearby Wijnbistro Patine *(Leopold de Waelstraat 1)* makes for a great pitstop as well.

TOP 10 ⭐ The Adoration of the Mystic Lamb

St Bavo's cathedral in Ghent is home to one of northern Europe's great cultural treasures. This exquisite polyptych, painted in 1432, is the masterpiece of brothers Hubrecht and Jan van Eyck. Its survival is a miracle. It was rescued from Protestant vandals in 1566, and from fire in 1822. Parts were taken by French soldiers in 1794, sold in 1816, then stolen in 1934. Following restoration, the polyptych is now on display in a state-of-the-art visitor centre opened in 2021.

1 The Polyptych
The painting consists of 12 panels **(above)**, four in the centre and four on each of the folding wings. The lower tier depicts the spirituality of the world, and God's chosen people; the upper tier shows the heavenly realm, with Adam and Eve on either end.

Plan of the Polyptych

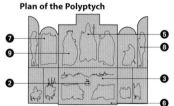

NEED TO KNOW

MAP Q2 ■ Sint-Baafskathedraal, Sint-Baafsplein ■ www.sint baafskathedraal.be

Open Altarpiece: 10am–5pm Mon–Sat, 1–5pm Sun; Cathedral: 8:30am–5:30pm Mon–Sat, 1–5:30pm Sun

Adm altarpiece & AR tour: €16 (€8 for under 12s); altarpiece: €12.50

■ There are many cafés nearby. Try the De Foyer café-restaurant in the Schouwburg (theatre), with a terrace overlooking the square (see p113).

■ Three different kinds of tours can be booked online, each for a duration of either 40 or 60 minutes.

■ All tours offer the chance to experience the polyptych in augmented reality by means of special AR glasses.

5 God the Almighty

The central figure of the upper tier is God, depicted in a brilliant red robe and a bejewelled mitre **(left)**, carrying a sceptre and with a crown at his feet. The benign calm and poise of the face radiate throughout the polyptych.

2 The Mystic Lamb of God

The focus of this panel **(below)** is the Lamb of God, spurting blood on an altar. It depicts four sets of figures approaching: virgin martyrs; figures from the New Testament and the Church; patriarchs and prophets of the Old Testament; and confessors of the Faith.

3 The Idealized City

To the rear of the central panel rise the towers and spires of the heavenly city of Jerusalem.

4 The Inscription

In the 19th century, a verse inscription by the two brothers, thought to be original, was uncovered on the frame.

INFLUENCE ON EUROPEAN ART

Flemish painters are sometimes credited with inventing oil painting. This is an exaggeration, but certainly they perfected the technique. Antonello da Messina, the Italian credited with pioneering oil painting in Italy, is believed to have learnt his skills from Flemish artists. As a result of this, the advantages of oil painting over tempera or fresco became clear. Italian artists adopted oil painting, and Italian art accelerated toward the High Renaissance.

8 Eve

Jan van Eyck's contemporaries were startled by the realism of his Adam and Eve. Even today, their nudity among the luxuriously clothed figures is striking **(left)**. They show the painter's great understanding of the human form.

6 Flowers

The numerous flowers make a philosophical point: everything in nature is an expression of God's work. The painter's job was to record it faithfully.

7 The Angel-Musicians

A heavenly choir sings on one side of the upper tier **(left)**, while on the other, an orchestra of angels plays. The figures are tightly crowded, but the perspective is good.

9 Mary

The figure of Mary tells us much about the concept of feminine beauty in medieval times. Fine-featured, absorbed in her reading, she is decked with jewels.

10 The External Panels

The wings of the painting can be closed. The external panels are tonally quite flat, intensifying the moment they are opened to reveal the sumptuous interior.

The Top 10
of Everything

**Beer on display at Huisbrouwerij
De Halve Maan, Bruges**

🔟 Moments in History

1 50s BC: Julius Caesar
The Roman army suffered repeated setbacks in its struggle against the courageous "Belgae", but Rome won out, and Belgium flourished under the Pax Romana of provincial rule for 400 years.

2 AD 843: Treaty of Verdun
After the Romans came the Franks, whose empire reached its apogee under Charlemagne. Following his death, his homeland was split by treaty along the River Scheldt – the division from which Flanders and Wallonia would evolve.

3 1302: Battle of the Golden Spurs
France dominated Flanders for much of the medieval period, resulting in popular revolt. At the Battle of the Golden Spurs, a Flemish rebel force humiliated the cream of the French army.

Battle of the Golden Spurs

4 1384: Burgundy Takes Over
When Louis de Male, Count of Flanders, died in 1384, his title was inherited by his son-in-law Philip the Bold (1342–1404), Duke of Burgundy. The dukes of Burgundy extended their control over the Low Countries.

Burgundian rule reached its peak under Philip the Good (r. 1419–67). Bruges, his capital, was the centre of a rich trading empire.

5 1568: Religious Strife
Charles V, Holy Roman Emperor and King of Spain, inherited the Burgundian territories, but faced violent opposition as Protestantism gathered pace. A decisive moment came in 1568, during the reign of Philip II, when counts Egmont and Hoorn were beheaded in the Grand Place for opposing the persecution of Protestants. Eventually the territory was divided into Protestant north (the Netherlands) and Catholic south (now Belgium).

6 1815: Battle of Waterloo
When the Spanish Netherlands passed to Austria in 1713, conservative groups began to agitate for Belgian independence. Their revolt was swept aside in 1794 when the French revolutionary armies invaded. The Belgians were divided over the merits of Napoleonic rule, and fought on both sides when Napoleon was defeated by the Allies at Waterloo *(see p69)*.

The Treaty of Verdun played a significant part in Belgian history

7 1830: The Belgian Revolution

Following Waterloo, the Congress of Vienna placed Belgium under Dutch rule, which was a deeply unpopular solution. Anger boiled over in 1830, independence was declared, and the Dutch army was forced out of Brussels.

Scenes from the Belgian Revolution

8 1914–18: World War I

At the outbreak of World War I, the German army swept into neutral Belgium. The Belgians thwarted their advance by flooding the land. The front settled near the medieval town of Ypres *(see p69)*. Over the next four years, half a million people from both sides died there.

9 1940–44: World War II

History was repeated in May 1940, when the German army launched a *Blitzkrieg* against neutral Belgium to outflank the Maginot Line, which blocked their entry into France. Brussels was liberated in September 1944.

10 1957: Treaty of Rome

Having been unwitting victims of two World Wars, the Belgians were enthusiastic supporters of the Treaty of Rome, which laid the foundations for the European Union. Over time, Brussels has effectively become the "Capital of Europe".

TOP 10 HISTORICAL FIGURES

1 Baldwin Iron-Arm
Baldwin (d. 879) became the first Count of Flanders, making Bruges his stronghold.

2 Pieter de Coninck and Jan Breydel
De Coninck, a weaver, and Breydel, a butcher, were instrumental in the successful Flemish rebellion against the French, launched in 1302.

3 Philip the Bold
Philip the Bold ushered in the Burgundian era in the Netherlands after inheriting control of Brussels and Flanders.

4 Philip the Good
Philip the Good founded the Order of the Golden Fleece and was a great patron of the arts.

5 Charles V
Born in Ghent, Charles V (1500–58) forged the largest empire in Europe since Roman times. His press is mixed.

6 Isabella and Albert
The dazzling court of the Infanta Isabella (1566–1633) and Archduke Albert (1559–1621) marked calmer times for Spanish Habsburg rule.

7 Charles of Lorraine
Austrian governor-general (r. 1744–80) credited with bringing the Age of Enlightenment to Brussels.

8 King Léopold I
First King of the Belgians (r. 1831–65), popular for his total commitment to the task.

9 King Léopold II
Second king of Belgium (r. 1865–1909) *(see p84)*.

10 Paul-Henri Spaak
Socialist prime minister from 1938 to 1939 and again during the post-war years, Spaak (1899–1972) played a central role in the creation of the European Community.

King Léopold I

🔟 Famous Belgians

Hergé at work illustrating Tintin inside a copy of his famous comic book

① Hergé

Georges Remi (1907–83) was a self-taught illustrator from the Brussels suburb of Etterbeek. In 1929 he published a story called *Tintin au Pays des Soviets*, and Belgium's most celebrated comic-strip character was born. Since then, 200 million Tintin books have been sold worldwide in some 50 languages. Georges Remi devised his pen name, Hergé, by simply reversing his initials and spelling out the sounds.

② Georges Simenon

One of the world's best-selling authors, Georges Simenon (1903–89) was born and raised in Liège. His most famous creation, the imperturbable Inspector Maigret, appeared in 75 of his 400-plus novels.

③ Gerard Mercator

Most school maps of the world are still based on the "Mercator projection" – an ingenious way of representing the spherical globe on a flat page. Mercator (1512–94) is also credited with creating the first "atlas", a word he introduced.

Gerard Mercator

④ Peyo

Born in Brussels, Pierre Culliford (1928–1992) was a comic-strip maestro who took on the pseudonym Peyo. He introduced the world to his famous cartoon creations, *The Smurfs*, in the late 1950s. Since then, his quirky, blue-skinned characters have featured in movies, TV shows, theme parks and video games.

⑤ Jacques Brel

Jacques Brel (1929–78) still ranks in many people's minds as the greatest singer-songwriter in the French language. Although he first made his name in France, he remained loyal to his Belgian origins. The Jacques Brel Foundation (*Place de la Vieille Halle aux Blés 11; www.jacquesbrel.be*) in Brussels celebrates his life and work.

⑥ Victor Horta

The Ghent-born architect and designer Victor Horta is credited with popularizing the Art Nouveau style in Belgium (see pp22–3). Designed by Horta, Hôtel Tassel (see p48) in Brussels is generally regarded as one of the first examples of Art

Nouveau building in Europe. With its curved forms, innovative use of iron, steel and glass and decorative nature-themed motifs, the hotel's open-plan interior heralded the design of modern architecture.

 Jean-Claude Van Damme

A former karate champion, Jean-Claude Van Damme (b. 1960) did odd jobs in California, such as delivering pizzas and laying carpets, before making his name with action thrillers including *Cyborg*, *Kickboxer* (1989) and *Universal Soldier* (1992).

8 Eddie Merckx

Cycling is a major sport in Belgium, and no name ranks higher than Eddie Merckx (b. 1945), five times winner of the Tour de France (from 1969–72 and in 1974).

Eddie Merckx in action

9 Justine Henin

One of the great women tennis players of the early 2000s, famed for her athletic grace on the court, Henin (b. 1982) won seven Grand Slam titles in her career. Her great Belgian rival Kim Clijsters won four.

10 Eden Hazard

One of a new generation of Belgian football stars, Hazard (b. 1991) has played for Chelsea, Lille and Belgium. His compatriots on the international football stage include Romelu Lukaku, Vincent Kompany and Thibaut Courtois.

TOP 10 OTHER FAMOUS BELGIANS

Jacky Ickx, Formula One legend

1 Andreas Vesalius
Physician to Charles V and Philip II of Spain, Vesalius (1514–64) was known as "the father of modern anatomy".

2 Adolphe Sax
Best known as inventor of the saxophone, Sax (1814–94) devised a range of other musical instruments.

3 Marie Popelin
The first Belgian female lawyer, Popelin (1846–1913) was not allowed to practise, so she devoted herself to fighting for women's rights.

4 Léo-Hendrik Baekeland
A great chemist (1863–1944) who invented Bakelite, the first totally synthetic plastic.

5 Henry van de Velde
Leading Art Nouveau designer (1863–1957) who laid the foundations for the Bauhaus movement.

6 Suzan Daniel
Founder of the country's LGBTQ+ movement and the first female Belgian film critic (1918–2007).

7 Jacky Ickx
Ickx was one of the great Formula One racing drivers of the 1960s and 1970s (b. 1945).

8 Anne Teresa De Keersmaeker
A leading choreographer (b. 1960) in the world of contemporary dance.

9 Dries van Noten
A celebrated fashion designer (b. 1958) who has helped bring Antwerp to the forefront of *haute couture*.

10 Matthias Schoenaerts
Film actor and heart-throb (b. 1977) who has achieved international acclaim in films including *Far from the Madding Crowd* (2015).

🔟 Belgian Artists

Altarpiece of the Seven Sacraments: Eucharist by Rogier van der Weyden

1 Rogier van der Weyden

Rogier van der Weyden (c.1400–64) was one of the leading Flemish "Primitives", and is best known for the intense emotion of his work, such as *The Seven Sacraments* in the Koninklijk Museum voor Schone Kunsten, Antwerp *(see p101)*. Working mainly in Brussels, he became the leading painter after the death of van Eyck.

2 Jan van Eyck

The sheer technical brilliance and almost photographic detail of work by Jan van Eyck (c.1390–1441) are self-evident in paintings such

Statue of van Eyck

as *Madonna with Canon Joris van der Paele (see p31)* and *The Adoration of the Mystic Lamb (see pp36–7)*. Van Eyck's work had a major impact on Italian art, and helped to fuel the Renaissance.

3 Hans Memling

Born in Germany, Hans Memling (c.1430–94) was probably trained by Rogier van der Weyden in Brussels before moving to Bruges. Memling went on to become one of the most successful artists of his day *(see pp30–31)*.

4 Pieter Bruegel the Elder

During the 16th century, Flemish artists turned to Italy for inspiration, which muddied their distinctive north European vision. But Pieter Bruegel (c.1525–69) rejected this trend and painted in a personal style based on what he saw around him. His depictions of rural villages generate a charm and honest naivety.

Rubens and Helene Fourment in the Garden (c. 1631), Rubens

5 Peter Paul Rubens

Almost all the best Flemish artists trained in Italy in the 16th century, and Peter Paul Rubens (1577–1640) used his experience to combine his prodigious Flemish technique with Italian flourish to produce art full of verve and dynamism.

6 Jacob Jordaens

After Rubens' death, another of his collaborators Jacob Jordaens

Four Doctors of the Church, **Jordaens**

(1593–1678) became Antwerp's leading painter. He is best remembered for allegorical paintings expressing the *joie-de-vivre* of the Baroque age.

7 Antoon van Dyck

Antoon van Dyck (1599–1641) was a colleague and friend of Rubens and matched many of the latter's skills, as well as addressing a similar range of subject matter. Van Dyck, however, is best known for his portraits. He became court painter to Charles I of England, who rewarded him with a knighthood.

8 James Ensor

The work of James Ensor (1860–1949) has earned him a reputation as one of art history's great eccentrics. His paintings incorporate skeletons, masks and hideous caricatures.

9 Paul Delvaux

Some memorable images of Surrealism came from the studio of Paul Delvaux (1897–1994). He is famous for his sensual, trance-like pictures of somnolent nudes in incongruous settings.

10 René Magritte

The dreamlike paintings of René Magritte (1898–1967) rank alongside Salvador Dalí's work as archetypal Surrealism. The Magritte Museum *(see p86)* displays paintings by the artist, plus photographs, drawings and archives.

TOP 10 OTHER BELGIAN ARTISTS

1 Clara Peeters
Known for her still-life works, Peeters (1594–1659) was one of the few professional women artists in the 17th century.

2 Constantin Meunier
Sculptor and painter (1831–1905) best-known for his bronzes of industrial workers *(see p85)*.

3 Émile Claus
Post-Impressionist painter (1849–1924) famous for rural scenes of sparkling clarity, achieved through a technique that he called "Luminism".

4 Jean Delville
One of the most inventive of the Symbolists (1867–1953), famed for colourful visions of Satanic forces.

5 Léon Spilliaert
Symbolist (1881–1946) of great originality, whose works, often black and white, are instantly recognizable.

6 Rik Wouters
A painter and sculptor (1882–1916) whose work is noted for being full of light, verve and charm.

7 Constant Permeke
A painter (1886–1952) of the second phase of the Sint-Martens-Latem school. His work has a social edge and dark, gritty textures.

8 Panamarenko
True to Surrealist traditions, this artist (1940–2019) was known for his mixed-media machinery sculptures.

9 Princess Delphine of Belgium
A royal artist and sculptor, Delphine Boël (b. 1968) is highly regarded for her controversial visual art.

10 Sergine André
This Haitian-Belgian artist (b. 1969) depicts her childhood homeland using bold, bright Expressionist designs.

Bords de la Lys (1920), **Émile Claus**

Churches

Nave of Sint-Salvatorskathedraal, Bruges' majestic cathedral

1 Cathédrale des Saints Michel et Gudule, Brussels

Brussels' honey-coloured Gothic cathedral is a sanctuary of calm after the bustle of the Grand Place. Used for royal weddings and funerals *(see p74)*.

2 Église Saint-Jacques-sur-Coudenberg, Brussels

MAP D4 ▪ Place Royale, 1000 BRU (Ixelles) ▪ 02 502 18 25 ▪ Open 1–5:45pm Wed–Sat, 8:30am–5:45pm Sun (till noon Jul–Aug)

This distinctive church occupies a prominent position overlooking the Place Royale. Its bell tower apart, it looks more like a Roman temple than a Christian church.

3 Église Notre-Dame du Sablon, Brussels

The 15th-century church of the Guild of Crossbowmen is an exemplar of Brabantine Gothic style, lit by large expanses of stained glass *(see p73)*.

4 Église Saint-Jean-Baptiste au Béguinage, Brussels

The lavish Flemish Baroque façade of this church contrasts with its history as the focal point of a *béguine* community of women *(see p75)*.

5 Sint-Salvators-kathedraal, Bruges

Both grand and sombre, the tone of this church befits its status as Bruges' cathedral. Although mainly Gothic, St Saviour's may date back in origin to early Christian times. The turreted tower was built in Neo-Medieval style in the late 19th century *(see p94)*.

6 Onze-Lieve-Vrouwekerk, Bruges

Bruges' most striking church, with a rocket-like spire built in the austere style of Scheldt Gothic. The interior has been tinkered with ceaselessly since the 13th century. Its outstanding treasure is Michelangelo's *Madonna and Child*, donated by a wealthy merchant in 1514 *(see p92)*.

7 Sint-Jacobskerk, Antwerp

The richly ornate interior of this church bears testimony to the fact that it was frequented by the well-to-do during Antwerp's

Tomb, Sint-Jacobskerk

17th-century heyday – among them was Rubens, who was buried in his family chapel here *(see p103)*.

8 Sint-Baafskathedraal, Ghent

The soaring Gothic interior and Baroque choir give Ghent's impressive cathedral a forceful quality *(see p109)*. It is upstaged, however, by its greatest treasure: Jan and Hubrecht van Eyck's magnificent *Adoration of the Mystic Lamb (see pp36–7)*.

9 Sint-Niklaaskerk, Ghent

The interior of Ghent's most attractive and imposing church has been scrubbed clean by a programme of restoration, resulting in a light and joyous space that makes the most of the robust Gothic stonework *(see p109)*.

Onze-Lieve-Vrouwekathedraal

10 Onze-Lieve-Vrouwekathedraal, Antwerp

With one of its two towers unfinished, Antwerp's cathedral bears the battle scars of its centuries-long struggle for completion, but the immense interior gives an indication of the scale of its creators' ambitions. It's also an apt setting for two stunning triptychs by Rubens *(see pp32–3)*.

TOP 10 ARCHITECTURAL STYLES

A perfect example of Gothic style

1 Romanesque
10th–12th centuries. Semi-circular arches and hefty columns. The style is called "Norman" in Britain.

2 Gothic
13th–16th centuries. Pointed arches allowed for lighter structures.

3 Scheldt (or Scaldian) Gothic
13th–14th centuries. An early, rather austere version of Gothic style, typical of that found in northern Belgium (around the River Scheldt).

4 Brabantine and Flamboyant Gothic
14th–15th centuries. A daintier form of Gothic, which is used for town halls such as Bruges' Stadhuis.

5 Renaissance
15th–17th centuries. An elegant style taking its inspiration from Greek and Roman architecture.

6 Baroque
17th–18th centuries. A lavish interpretation of Classical style, full of exuberance and swagger.

7 Neo-Classical
18th–19th centuries. Another Classical style that took inspiration from Greek and Roman temples.

8 Neo-Gothic
19th-century. A Gothic-inspired style revisited that was adopted particularly by the Catholic Revival.

9 Art Nouveau
Late 19th–early 20th centuries. A florid, organic style, intended to create an utterly new approach: hence "new art".

10 Art Deco
1920s–1930s. A brash, angular but glamorous style. Name is based on a 1925 decorative arts exhibition in Paris.

TOP 10 Art Nouveau Buildings in Brussels

Inside the Horta Museum

1 Horta Museum
The former home and studio of the great maestro of Art Nouveau architecture, Victor Horta, serves as a masterclass in the art *(see pp22–3)*.

2 Hôtel Tassel
Rue Paul-Émile Janson 6, 1050 BRU (Ixelles)
Designed by Victor Horta in 1892–3, this is considered the first Art Nouveau house. Up to this point, the well-to-do who commissioned new private mansions in the mushrooming Belgian suburbs adopted any style, going from Moorish to Medieval or Tuscan. Horta extrapolated from this "eclectic" style to evolve something more integrated and considered. The private mansion of a bachelor engineer, Hôtel Tassel was carefully tailored to all aspects of his lifestyle, but this individualized approach also made it less adaptable for subsequent owners.

3 Hôtel Saint-Cyr
Square Ambiorix 11, 1000 BRU (Brussels)
Art Nouveau tended toward excess, and is taken to glorious extreme at this house – all loops and curves, with a circular picture window on the top floor. It was designed for painter Saint-Cyr in 1900.

4 Hôtel Hannon
MAP G2 ■ Avenue de la Jonction 1, 1060 BRU (Saint-Gilles)
Built in 1903–4, this was a private mansion designed by Jules Brunfaut for Édouard Hannon, an industrialist, painter and photographer with a keen interest in Art Nouveau. The stained-glass windows were designed by glassmaker Raphaël Évaldre, who trained at Tiffany's.

5 Comics Art Museum
Victor Horta designed the Magasins Waucquez, a textile shop, in 1903. Rescued in the 1970s, it has found new life as the famous comic museum *(see pp26–7)*.

6 La Maison Cauchie
Rue des Francs 5, 1040 BRU (Etterbeek) ■ 02 733 86 84 ■ Open 10am–1pm, 2–5pm first Sat & Sun of month ■ Adm
Behind a façade of geometric shapes with dreamy Art Nouveau murals lies the 1905 home of little-known painter Paul Cauchie (1875–1952).

The façade of La Maison Cauchie

7 Musée des Instruments de Musique, Brussels

Art Nouveau was also called "Style Liberty", after the famous London store. Brussels' "Old England" store was named to echo this vogue. The building now houses the Museum of Musical Instruments *(see pp20–21)*.

8 Le Falstaff
MAP B3 ■ Rue Henri Maus 19, 1000 BRU (Brussels) ■ 02 511 87 89

This famous brasserie-restaurant opposite the Bourse dates from 1903, and still powerfully evokes the era in which it was created. The interior is rich in Art Nouveau detail.

Wonderfully ornate Le Falstaff

9 Hôtel Solvay
Avenue Louise 224, 1050 BRU (Ixelles)

The 33-year-old Victor Horta was still fairly unknown when he was commissioned to design this house by the industrialist Ernest Solvay. Its free-flowing form, with swirling wrought iron and a remarkably fluid use of stonework, established Horta as a master of the Art Nouveau style.

10 Hôtel Ciamberlani
Rue Defacqz 48, 1050 BRU (Ixelles)

The artist Albert Ciamberlani (1864–1956) was one of those responsible for the huge mural in the triumphal colonnade of the Cinquantenaire building *(see p51)*. He employed Paul Hankar (1859–1901), a key Art Nouveau architect, to build his house and studio in 1897. The façade combines iron, stone and brick for a highly individual decorative effect.

TOP 10 ARCHITECTURAL WONDERS

MAS, Antwerp

1 Jeruzalemkapel, Bruges
A Byzantine-influenced church inspired by a pilgrimage to the Holy Land *(see p95)*.

2 Palais de Justice, Brussels
Joseph Poelaert threw every Neo-Classical style in the book at this domineering monument to justice *(see p76)*.

3 Pavillon Chinois, Tour Japonaise, Brussels
MAP G1
Two beautiful Asian-influenced buildings rising from the Parc de Laeken.

4 Serres Royales, Brussels
Magnificent royal greenhouses built in the 1870s *(see p86)*.

5 Havenhuis, Antwerp
The new Port House (2009–16), designed by British-Iraqi architect Zaha Hadid.

6 Centraal Station, Antwerp
Louis Delacenserie's station is a potpourri of Neo-Classical styles *(see p65)*.

7 The Palais Stoclet, Brussels
MAP H2 ■ Avenue de Tervuren 281, 1150 BRU (Woluwe Saint-Pierre)
Designed by Josef Hoffmann, and with murals by Gustav Klimt, this private mansion was an architectural shocker.

8 MAS, Antwerp
A striking and innovative museum, completed in 2011 *(see p102)*.

9 The Atomium, Brussels
A giant model of a crystal of iron, created for the 1958 Universal Exposition *(see p83)*.

10 Basilique Nationale du Sacré-Coeur, Brussels
There is something strangely soulless about this massive 20th-century church *(see p86)*.

📖 Museums

1 Musées Royaux d'Art et d'Histoire, Brussels

Belgium's collection of historic national and international treasures is housed in this palatial building. It includes an impressive array of medieval church treasures (in the Salle aux Trésors), tapestries, Art Nouveau sculpture and jewellery, antique costumes and archaeological finds. One of three museums in the Parc du Cinquantenaire (see p84).

Treasures at Musée Charlier, Brussels

2 Musée des Instruments de Musique, Brussels

Housed in a classic Art Nouveau department store, perched on a ridge, "Le mim" is one of Brussels' must-see sights. More than 1,200 multifarious exhibits are enhanced by listening to their sounds on an iPad-like device (see pp20–21).

3 Volkskundemuseum, Bruges

See life as it was lived by the ordinary folk of Bruges in the often threadbare 19th and early 20th centuries. Fascinating collections of household items, as well as complete workshops, bring home the extraordinary changes of the last century and a half (see p95).

Folk artifacts at Volkskundemuseum

4 Musée Charlier, Brussels

A rare opportunity to see inside one of Brussels' maisons de maître (mansions). As well as a fine collection of antique furniture, the Hôtel Charlier contains many reminders of its days as a meeting place for the avant-garde set in the early 20th century (see p74).

5 Museum Aan de Stroom (MAS), Antwerp

This dynamic construction of perspex and red sandstone is packed with ethnographic and folkloric treasures – plus there are great city views from the rooftop (see p102).

An exhibit at Museum Aan de Stroom, Antwerp

6 Gruuthusemuseum, Bruges

For over 100 years this historic house has served as a museum presenting an ever-growing collection of artifacts. From tapestries and Gothic stained-glass windows to porcelain and silver items, the collection spans Bruges' medieval heyday to the 19th century.

THE CINQUANTENAIRE

Parc du Cinquantenaire arch

The era of great international fairs was launched by the Great Exhibition in Hyde Park, London, in 1851. King Léopold II decided to mount a similar exhibition to mark the 50th anniversary *(cinquantenaire)* of the founding of Belgium in 1880. The site chosen was marshland to the east of the historic centre of Brussels. A pair of exhibition complexes, linked by a monumental semi-circular colonnade, was commissioned from Gédéon Bordiau. The project was not completed in time for the 1880 jubilee, but building continued, and the site was used for subsequent fairs. The central triumphal arch – topped by a quadriga reminiscent of the one on Berlin's Brandenburg Gate – was completed in 1905 to mark Belgium's 75th anniversary. Bordiau's barrel-vaulted exhibition hall houses the Musée Royal de l'Armée et d'Histoire Militaire. Its twin to the south was destroyed by fire in 1946; its replacement now forms part of the Musées Royaux d'Art et d'Histoire. The Parc and Palais du Cinquantenaire also contain Autoworld *(see p84)*, as well as two curiosities: the Atelier de Moulage and the Pavillon Horta-Lambeaux *(see p84)*.

⑦ Horta Museum, Brussels

The full artistic potential of Art Nouveau is apparent in this museum, which was formerly the house and offices of Victor Horta, the father of Art Nouveau architecture *(see pp22–3)*.

⑧ Design Museum Gent, Ghent

This delightful decorative museum *(see p111)* follows changing styles from the domestic elegance of the 17th century to the jocular irreverence of Milanese Post-Modernism. It is currently closed for renovation and expansion until 2024.

⑨ Huis van Alijn, Ghent

Set in picturesque almshouses founded by the Alijn family in the 14th century, this museum is a repository for a huge range of artifacts that were part and parcel of the lives of ordinary Flemish people in both recent times and in the past centuries *(see p110)*.

Museum Plantin-Moretus, Antwerp

⑩ Museum Plantin-Moretus, Antwerp

Within a century of Gutenberg's breakthrough in European printing by means of movable type, this 16th-century printing house (now a UNESCO World Heritage Site) had become a leader of the publishing revolution. Visitors can view historic printing presses and engraving plates in the workshop *(see p102)*.

TOP10 Art Galleries

The Village Lawyer (1621) by Pieter Brueghel the Younger at MSK, Ghent

1 Museum voor Schone Kunsten (MSK), Ghent

Ghent's museum of fine arts is a bit of a mixed bag, but has a handful of outstanding pieces; just a stone's throw from SMAK *(see p111)*.

2 Musée d'Ixelles, Brussels

This small but rewarding collection features names such as Magritte, Rembrandt, Toulouse-Lautrec and Picasso, as well as leading Belgian artists including Léon Spilliaert. The museum is closed for renovation until 2024.

3 Koninklijk Museum voor Schone Kunsten (KMSKA), Antwerp

One of the great European collections, the Royal Museum of Fine Arts features works by Old Masters including Rubens and Van Dyck and modernists such as James Ensor and Rik Wouters *(see pp34–5)*.

4 Musées Royaux des Beaux-Arts, Brussels

Brussels' royal museum of fine art holds rich collections of such artists as Bruegel, Rubens and Jordaens. Outstanding 19th-century art and Art Nouveau is shown in the separate but integrated Fin-de-Siècle Museum, and the Magritte Museum next door has a comprehensive collection of the great Surrealist's work *(see pp18–19)*.

5 Meunier Museum, Brussels

The suburban home of the late-19th-century sculptor Constantin Meunier has been turned into a gallery devoted to his work; it leaves visitors in no doubt of his gifts and the punch of his social criticism *(see p85)*.

6 Van Buuren Museum, Brussels

A private collection of art is presented in its original setting: a charming Art Deco home with a beautiful garden *(see p83)*.

Koninklijk Museum, Antwerp

Groeningemuseum, Bruges

Bruges' main gallery is celebrated for its collection of paintings by Flemish Masters of the late medieval era. A small, easily digestible museum *(see pp30–31)*.

8 Sint-Janshospitaal, Bruges

A superb collection of paintings by Flemish Primitive Hans Memling was originally commissioned for the chapel of this medieval hospital to bring solace to the sick. The conjoining wards and chapel have been restored, giving these works a fascinating context *(see pp30–31)*.

9 Stedelijk Museum voor Actuele Kunst (SMAK), Ghent

This acclaimed gallery of contemporary art not only mounts cutting-edge temporary exhibitions, but also has a remarkable permanent collection. The works on display are guaranteed to provoke a reaction from aficionados and the unconverted alike *(see p111)*.

MUHKA, Antwerp

10 Museum van Hedendaagse Kunst (MUHKA), Antwerp

The location of this contemporary art gallery, in the up-and-coming former dockland area in the south of the city, sets the tone for what lies inside. A ground-breaking museum *(see p104)*.

TOP 10 WORKS OUTSIDE GALLERIES

A replica of Rodin's *The Thinker*

1 The Adoration of the Mystic Lamb (1432), Ghent
Jan and Hubrecht van Eyck's masterpiece *(see pp36–7)*.

2 Madonna and Child (1504–5)
Michelangelo's sculpture of mesmeric dignity *(see p92)* in Bruges.

3 The Raising of the Cross (1609–10)
Wonderful triptych in Antwerp by Pieter Paul Rubens *(see p34)*.

4 The Descent from the Cross (1611–14), Antwerp
Rubens' triptych contrasts Christ's death with the Nativity *(see p34)*.

5 Baroque Pulpit (1699)
Hendrik Verbruggen's elaborate carved pulpit in Brussels' cathedral *(see pp74–5)*.

6 The History of Bruges (1895)
In the Stadhuis of Bruges *(see pp28–9)*, 12 superb Neo-Medievalist murals by Albert and Julien De Vriendt.

7 Fountain of Kneeling Youths (1898)
Emile Braunplein (in front of the Belfort, Ghent)
George Minne's best-known work.

8 The Thinker (c.1905)
MAP F1 ▪ Parvis Notre-Dame, 1020 BRU (Laeken) ▪ Open 8:30am–4:30pm daily
A copy of Rodin's statue on a tomb in Laeken Cemetery, Brussels.

9 Nos Vieux Trams Bruxellois (1978)
Bourse Station, Brussels
Paul Delvaux's contribution to putting art in the metro.

10 Hergé Mural (1983)
MAP H2 ▪ Stockel Metro, Brussels
A cartoon mural decorating Stockel metro station by Hergé.

🔟 Off the Beaten Track

Église St-Jean-Baptiste au Béguinage, Brussels

1 Église St-Jean-Baptiste au Béguinage, Brussels

This understated Baroque church was once at the heart of an extensive *béguinage (see box p92)*, and still provides tranquillity for visitors close to the heart of the city *(see p75)*.

2 Brussels Comic Book Route

www.brussels.be/comic-book-route

The self-proclaimed comic book capital of the world has around 50 murals of popular characters installed across the city. The murals pay tribute to favourites, such as Tintin, Snowy and Captain Haddock *(Rue de la'Etuve 37)*, cowboy Lucky Luke *(Rue de la Buanderie 40)* and prankster Gaston Lagaffe *(Rue de l'Ecuyer 11)*. There is also a huge wall display of Asterix and Obelix *(Rue de la Buanderie 33)*.

3 Maison Autrique, Brussels

This large and grand private mansion, in the northern suburb of Schaerbeek, was designed by Victor Horta in 1893. It was his first project, just before he really embraced the Art Nouveau style. The mansion, from the cellar kitchen to the attic, has been restored and furnished in original style so that visitors can view the furnishings and decor of late 19th-century life *(see p86)*.

4 Van Buuren Museum, Brussels

Head out to the southern suburb of Uccle to find the comfortable 1920s Art Deco home and gardens of David and Alice van Buuren. They surrounded themselves with a superb collection of art by many of the leading Belgian and European artists, both historic and contemporary *(see p83)*.

5 Patershol, Ghent

MAP Q1

Behind the Huis van Alijn folk museum *(see p110)* is a warren of cobbled streets, once the heart of medieval Ghent and home to leatherworkers and Carmelite Friars (Paters). In the 17th and 18th centuries, magistrates working at the nearby fortress, the Gravensteen, lived here, which accounts for some of the grander houses, but during Ghent's industrialisation in the 19th century the area became a notorious slum. Restoration began in the 1980s and the Patershol has now been pedestrianized and gentrified, but it still retains its historical charm.

Charming Patershol district, Ghent

6 Eastern Bruges

Most visitors to Bruges frequent the centre and southwest of the city. Head east for peace and quiet, and a collection of interesting churches and museums *(see p95)*.

Galerie Bortier, Brussels

7 Galerie Bortier, Brussels

Time stands still among the second-hand books and prints on sale beneath the glass canopies of this 1847 shopping arcade *(see p77)*.

8 Maison d'Érasme and Béguinage d'Anderlecht, Brussels

These two enchanting museums, in the western suburb of Anderlecht, are close enough together to be visited in a single trip *(see p86)*.

9 Muur der Doodgeschotenen, Bruges
MAP M3

At the site of a former barracks on the Kazernevest, in eastern Bruges, a bullet-marked brick wall and a line of monuments commemorates the place where a dozen men were executed by the German army during World War I. The one British victim was Captain Fryatt, a merchant navy officer, whose death became a *cause célèbre* at the time.

10 Begijnhof, Antwerp
MAP U1 ■ Rodestraat 39
■ Open 8am–6pm daily

A place of therapeutic calm, Antwerp's *béguinage* (*begijnhof* in Dutch) was built originally in 1545, and is still used as housing.

TOP 10 BEST PARKS AND OPEN SPACES

1 Parc de Bruxelles (Warande)
MAP D3
Lovely formal park laid out in the 18th century, in front of the Palais Royal.

2 Place du Petit Sablon, Brussels
A tiny park famous for its statues of medieval guildworkers *(see p73)*.

3 Parc d'Egmont, Brussels
MAP C5
A green oasis close to the Avenue Louise shopping hub.

4 Étangs d'Ixelles, Brussels
MAP G2
Two large ponds, good for a stroll or a picnic when visiting the Horta Museum and the Art Nouveau district.

5 Forêt de Soignes, Brussels
The great beech forest to the south of the city *(see p68)*.

6 Minnewater, Bruges
The so-called "Lake of Love", with surrounding park, in the south of Bruges *(see p94)*.

7 Koningin Astridpark, Bruges
MAP L4
This former monastery garden is now a park with children's play equipment. The park was featured in the 2008 film *In Bruges*.

8 Citadelpark, Ghent
MAP P6
A great park with Ghent's main art galleries; on the city's southern edge.

9 Stadspark, Antwerp
MAP U3
A triangular green lung, southeast of the centre of Antwerp.

10 Middelheim Museum, Antwerp
A rewarding open-air sculpture park *(see p104)*.

Minnewater in autumn, Bruges

Children's Attractions

The "Mini-Europe" in Bruparck, near the Atomium

1 Bruparck, Brussels

MAP F1 ▪ Bvd du Centenaire 20, 1020 BRU ▪ 02 474 83 83 ▪ Opening times vary; check website for details ▪ Adm ▪ www.bruparck.com

Near the Atomium *(see p82)* this huge recreational area has several family-friendly amusements including a cinema and "Mini-Europe".

2 Antwerp Zoo

MAP V2 ▪ Koningin Astridplein 26 ▪ 03 202 45 40 ▪ Open 10am–5:30pm daily (closing times vary between 4:45 & 7pm) ▪ Adm ▪ www.zooantwerpen.be

One of the oldest zoos in the world (1843), it is also a centre for research and conservation. Special attractions include penguin-feeding, elephant bathing, a hippo pond as well as a hands-on reptile experience.

3 Comics Art Museum, Brussels

Older children will be intrigued by this unusual museum; younger children may not be, especially if they speak neither French nor Dutch *(see pp26–7).*

Snowy, Comics Art Museum

4 Historic Tram Ride, Brussels

This fun tram ride should appeal to children of all ages. A vintage tram strains and squeaks its way along a 40-km (25-mile) circuit of wooded paths from the Musée du Tram *(see p86).* It operates on Sunday mornings from April to September.

5 Illusion Brussels

Enjoy the fun world of illusions and special effects with your family in this small but highly-entertaining interactive museum *(see p76).*

6 Manneken-Pis Costume Collection, Brussels

You may be lucky to find the Mannekin-Pis *(see p16)* on one of his dressed-up days. In any case, it's always fun to see his wardrobe in the Maison du Roi *(see p15),* where about 100 of his 815 outfits are on display.

7 Belfort, Bruges

A kind of medieval theme-park experience: the physical challenge of a slightly scary spiral staircase, magnificent views from the top, and a bit of a shock if the bells ring while you are up there. There may be a queue to get in *(see p91)*.

8 Walibi Belgium

Wavre ■ Walibi Belgium: 01 042 15 00. Aqualibi: 01 042 16 03 ■ Opening times vary; check website for details ■ Adm ■ www.walibi.com

Belgium's premier amusement park has everything, from scary roller coasters and vertical drops to soak-to-the-skin water rides, including more gentle, traditional-tracked car rides and roundabouts for younger visitors. There is also a multi-pool swimming complex, called Aqualibi, with a host of shoots and tube-runs.

Boat trip on a canal in Bruges

9 Canal Boat Trips, Bruges and Ghent

From a canal boat the landmarks of Bruges and Ghent show themselves in a new light. Boats leave from various spots in the centre of Bruges and from the Graslei and Korenlei in Ghent *(see p109)*.

10 Boudewijn Seapark, Bruges

Alfons De Baeckestraat 12, 8200 Sint-Michiels ■ 050 38 38 38 ■ Opening times vary; check website for details ■ Adm ■ www.boudewijnseapark.be

Bruges' amusement park, in a suburb to the south of the city, features marine-themed rides and attractions, such as an orca-themed roller coaster and an aqua park with slides and water fountains.

TOP 10 OTHER SIGHTS FOR CHILDREN

1 Pixel Museum, Brussels
Play vintage video games as well as the latest releases here *(see p84)*.

2 mim, Brussels
Music in the headphones changes as you go around *(see pp20–21)*.

3 Muséum des Sciences Naturelles, Brussels
Good for the scientist, ecologist and dinosaur fanatic *(see p86)*.

4 Musée des Enfants, Brussels
Rue du Bourgmestre 15, 1050 BRU (Ixelles) ■ 02 640 01 07
Popular museum for children aged 4–12. Limited numbers.

5 Choco-Story, Brussels
MAP B3 ■ Rue de l'Etuve 41, 1000 BRU ■ 02 514 20 48 ■ Open 10am–6pm daily (last entry 5pm) ■ Adm ■ www.choco-story-brussels.be
See and taste chocolate in the making.

6 Théâtre Royale du Péruchet, Brussels
MAP G2 ■ 50 Avenue de la Fôret, 1050 BRU (Ixelles) ■ Shows: 3pm Wed, Sat & Sun ■ www.theatre peruchet.be
Long-established puppet theatre and museum with shows specifically for children aged 3 and above.

7 Waterloo, Brussels
The battlefield has a visitor centre and various outlying museums *(see p69)*.

8 Historium, Bruges
Multimedia history of medieval Bruges *(see p94)*.

9 Huis van Alijn, Ghent
Magical folk museum *(see p110)*.

10 Het Gravensteen, Ghent
This heavily restored medieval castle is complete with dungeons *(see p111)*.

Het Gravensteen, Ghent

🔟 Performing Arts Venues

Théâtre Royal de la Monnaie, Brussels

The largest of the three concert halls can accommodate an impressive 2,000 visitors.

1 Théâtre Royal de la Monnaie, Brussels

MAP C2 ▪ Place de la Monnaie, 1000 BRU ▪ 02 229 12 11 (for tickets) ▪ www.lamonnaie.be

The most revered performing arts venue in the country, La Monnaie (Dutch: De Munt) is celebrated as the place where the Revolution of 1830 (see p41) began when a crowd took to the streets incited by Auber's opera *La Muette de Portici*. It was rebuilt in Neo-Classical style in 1819; the interior was redesigned after a fire in 1855.

2 Palais des Beaux-Arts, Brussels (BOZAR)

MAP D4 ▪ Rue Ravenstein 23, 1000 BRU ▪ 02 507 82 00 ▪ www.bozar.be

Victor Horta's Palais des Beaux-Arts was completed in 1928. Known as BOZAR, it is a multi-arts venue, covering music, theatre and more.

3 Ancienne Belgique, Brussels

MAP B3 ▪ Boulevard Anspach 110, 1000 BRU ▪ www.abconcerts.be

This well-established venue for pop as well as rock concerts, in central Brussels, presents interesting and high-profile acts.

4 Les Halles de Schaerbeek, Brussels

MAP G2 ▪ Rue Royale Sainte-Marie 22a, 1030 BRU (Schaerbeek) ▪ 02 218 21 07 ▪ www.halles.be

The magnificent old covered market, built in iron and glass at the end of the 19th century, has been transformed into an inspirational venue for a variety of cultural events – including drama, dance and music.

5 Concertgebouw, Bruges

MAP J5 ▪ 't Zand 34 ▪ 070 22 12 12 ▪ www.concertgebouw.be

As part of its celebrations as the Cultural Capital of Europe in 2002, Bruges created a new concert hall. The result is a highly innovative building that quickly became established as a leading venue for classical music, as well as ballet and jazz.

6 Théâtre Royal de Toone, Brussels

MAP C3 ▪ Rue du Marché aux Herbes 66 (Impasse Sainte Pétronille), 1000 BRU ▪ 02 511 71 37 ▪ www.toone.be

Théâtre Royal de Toone

The Toone marionette theatre, occupying a tiny building at the bottom of a medieval alley, is a Brussels institution. Note that this is not for children: the plays – enacted by traditional puppets made of wood and papier-mâché – may be serious classics of theatre, and the language is often Bruxellois, the rich dialect of the city. You can also visit the museum of retired puppets.

7 De Vlaamse Opera, Ghent

MAP Q3 ■ Schouwburgstraat 3
■ 070 22 02 02 ■ www.operaballet.be
This classic opera house – the Ghent home of the much-respected Vlaamse Opera Company – ranks among the most spectacular theatres in Europe.

8 De Vlaamse Opera, Antwerp

MAP U2 ■ Frankrijklei 3 ■ 070 22 02 02 ■ www.operaballet.be
Antwerp's opera house was completed in 1907, with its interior elegantly decked out with marble and gilding. The Vlaamse Opera Company also performs here.

Le Botanique, Brussels

9 Le Botanique, Brussels

MAP D1 ■ Rue Royale 236, 1210 BRU (Saint-Josse-ten-Noode)
■ 02 218 37 32 ■ www.botanique.be
The beautiful glasshouses of Brussels' botanical gardens were built between 1826 and 1829. Conversion of the interior has created what is now a key venue for a wide range of cultural activities, including theatre, dance and concerts.

10 deSingel, Antwerp

Desguinlei 25 ■ 03 248 28 28
■ www.desingel.be
This vibrant multi-purpose cultural centre is a venue for performances and exhibitions of drama, dance, architecture and music.

TOP 10 BELGIAN WRITERS, POETS AND MUSICIANS

Django Reinhardt and his band

1 Roland de Lassus
Also known as Orlando di Lasso (c.1532–94). One of the leading composers of his day.

2 César Franck
Organist and composer (1822–90) in the Romantic tradition.

3 Émile Verhaeren
Symbolist poet (1855–1916) noted for his portrayals (in French) of Flanders.

4 Maurice Maeterlinck
Nobel-Prize-winning Symbolist poet and dramatist (1862–1949).

5 Michel de Ghelderode
Belgium's most celebrated 20th-century playwright (1898–1962), and one of the most original writers in the French language.

6 Georges Simenon
Prolific master of the popular detective story (1903–89) and creator of Inspector Maigret *(see p42)*.

7 Django Reinhardt
The most celebrated jazz guitarist, Reinhardt (1910–53) was a member of the Quintet of the Hot Club of France.

8 Arthur Grumiaux
A leading violinist of his era (1921–86).

9 Liliane Wouters
The lyrical poetry of this poet and playwright (1930–2016), written in both French and Dutch, represents the two cultures of Belgium.

10 Amélie Nothomb
One of Belgium's most successful modern novelists (b. 1966), noted for her exploration of the darker sides of human nature.

🔟 Types of Belgian Beer

1 Witbier/Bière Blanche
Most beer is made from barley, but it can also be made from wheat to produce a distinctive "white beer" to which flavourings such as coriander and orange peel may be added. The result is a light, sparkling and refreshing beer, often served cloudy with sediment. Examples include Hoegaarden and Brugs.

2 Kriek
Lambic (see opposite page) can be flavoured with cherries (formerly the cherries of the north Brussels orchards of Schaerbeek), added during fermentation to create a highly distinctive drink called *kriek*. With raspberries it makes *framboise*; with candy sugar it makes *faro*. Of the three, newcomers may find *faro* the easiest to begin with.

3 Strong Ales
Some breweries pride themselves on the sheer power of their product. Duvel ("Devil"), at 8.5 per cent, is a famous example. Several lay claim to being the strongest beer in Belgium; at 12 per cent, Bush beer is a contender, and to be treated with respect.

4 Trappist Beer
In the past, some of Belgium's finest beers were made by the Trappists, a silent order of Cistercian monks. Now it's produced commercially by five breweries with close ties to the monasteries (Chimay, Westmalle, Orval, Rochefort and Westvleteren). Yeast is added at bottling to induce a second fermentation; it is important to pour off carefully in one go to avoid disturbing the sediment.

A bottle of *kriek*

5 Abbey Beer
Other abbeys also produced beer but, unlike the Trappist monasteries, many have licensed them to commercial breweries. Leffe, for example, is now owned by AB InBev. That said, many of the abbey beers are excellent. In addition, there are good "abbey-style" beers, such as Ename, Floreffe and St Feuillien.

6 Double/Triple
Traditionally, breweries graded their beers by strength: apparently single was around 3 per cent, double 6 per cent and triple 9 per cent. Some breweries – notably the Abbeys – still label their beers double *(dubbel)* and triple *(tripel)*. Double is usually a dark and sweetish brew, triple often golden-blond.

7 Lager-Style Beers
The *Pilsner*, or lager, is a bottom-fermented beer: the yeast remains at the bottom of the brew

Orval Abbey, famous for its Trappist beer produced by the monks

(stronger, heavier ales tend to be top-fermented, which seals in more flavour). Although such light beers may be sniffed at by connoisseurs in other countries; in Belgium they are brewed to a high standard. Despite its ubiquity, AB InBev's famous Stella Artois, brewed in Leuven, is a good-quality lager.

Barrels of fermenting beer, Lambic

8 Lambic

In the valley of the Senne, the river that flows through Brussels, there is a natural air-borne yeast called *Brettanomyces*. For centuries, brewers have simply left their warm wheat-beer wort uncovered during the winter months, and allowed air to deliver the yeast into it. The fermenting beer is then left to mature in wooden casks for a year or more. This creates a very distinctive beer, with a slightly winey edge, called *lambic* – the quint-essential beer of Brussels.

9 Gueuze

Lambic of various ages can be blended, and then fermented a second time in the bottle. This produces a beer called *gueuze*, which is fizzy like champagne and matured a further year or two to accentuate the wine-like qualities of the original product.

10 Christmas Beers

Many of the breweries produce Christmas ales for the festive season. These may just be prettily labelled versions of their usual brew, but they may also be enriched ales of high strength.

TOP 10 CLASSIC BELGIAN DISHES

1 Carbonnades Flamandes/ Vlaamse Stoverij
A beef stew cooked in Belgian beer – rich, succulent and sweet, and best eaten with *frites* and mayonnaise.

2 Jets d'Houblon
Hop-shoots – a springtime by-product of brewing – usually served in a cream sauce. They taste a bit like asparagus.

3 Waterzooi
A creamy, comforting dish of chicken (or fish) with vegetables in broth; a traditional dish of Ghent.

4 Chicons au Gratin
Belgian endives wrapped in ham and baked in a creamy cheese sauce.

5 Anguilles au Vert/ Paling in 't Groen
Freshwater eels cooked in a thick sauce of fresh green herbs.

6 Garnaalkroketten
Deep-fried potato croquettes filled with fresh shrimps; they make an excellent starter or snack.

7 Salade Liégeoise
A warm salad of potatoes and green beans, or *salade frisée*, with fried bacon bits.

8 Stoemp
Mashed potato mixed with a vegetable, such as carrots, leeks or celeriac.

9 Flamiche aux Poireaux
A quiche-like tart, made with leeks.

10 Moules marinière
Mussels, steamed until they open, in white wine flavoured with celery, onion and parsley; usually served in something resembling a bucket, accompanied by a plate of *frites*.

Moules marinière

TOP 10 Things to Buy

Antiques and bric-a-brac for sale at Place du Jeu de Balle in Brussels

1 Antiques and Bric-a-brac

For lovers of everything from old comics and Art Nouveau door handles to exquisite Louis XVI desks and ormolu clocks, Belgium is a happy hunting ground. In Brussels, the full range is on view between the Place du Jeu de Balle and the Place du Grand Sablon (see p77).

2 Chocolate

Belgian chocolate is justly famous for its smooth, delicious taste. The manufacturers use high-quality cocoa beans and reintroduce a generous proportion of cocoa butter. They also invented the means to manufacture filled chocolates (or pralines) on an industrial scale. As a result, these superb chocolates are remarkably good value.

3 Beer

In 1900 there were over 3,200 breweries in Belgium; now there are just over 150, but they still generate an astonishing variety of beers (see pp60–61). The most famous, and also some of the finest, are produced by the Trappist monasteries, but even the lighter, lager-style beers such as Stella Artois and Jupiler are made to a high standard. There are specialist beer shops in all the main cities.

4 Biscuits and Pâtisserie

It is hard not to drool in front of the ravishing shop windows of Belgian pâtisseries – and the mouthwatering offerings usually taste as good as they look. An alternative is to buy some of the equally famed biscuits from a specialist such as Dandoy (see p17).

5 Tapestry

Tapestry was one of the great medieval industries of Brussels and Bruges. It is still made on a craft basis, but of course large pieces come at luxury prices.

6 Lace

There were tens of thousands of lace-makers in 19th-century Belgium, many of them living in penury. That industry was undermined by the invention of lace-making

Exquisite Belgian handmade lace

machines, and to some degree it still is. If you want to buy handmade Belgian lace, go to a reputable shop, insist on a label of authenticity, and expect a high price.

7 Haute Couture

Since the 1980s, Belgium has shot to the forefront of the fashion world, with designers such as Dries van Noten, Raf Simons and Walter van Beirendonck. Many of the major designers have their own shops in Antwerp (see p105), but there are plenty of outlets in the Rue Antoine Dansaert in Brussels (see p77).

8 Children's Clothes

There are numerous shops devoted to children's clothes in Belgium, and their products are irresistible – from hard-wearing romp-around cottons to beautifully made winter jackets and hats, and unusual, fun shoes.

9 Tintin Merchandise

Tintin fans can pick up not only the books, but also T-shirts, figurines, games, postcards, mobile phone covers, key rings, stationery, mugs – you name it. The characters are copyrighted, so high-quality, legally produced goods come at a fairly steep price. There is a dedicated Tintin shop in Rue de la Colline, Brussels.

Tintin figure

10 Diamonds

HRD: www.hrdantwerp.com

Over three-quarters of the world's uncut diamonds flow through the exchanges of Antwerp; many of these are cut, polished and mounted there. You could find some bargains – but of course, you have to know what you're doing. If in doubt, consult the Hoge Raad voor Diamant (HRD), which oversees a reliable system of certification.

TOP 10 SUPPLIERS OF CHOCOLATES, BISCUITS AND PÂTISSERIE

Chocolate strawberries at Godiva

1 Godiva
www.godivachocolates.eu
Maker of luxury chocolates, with branches worldwide.

2 Marijn Coertjens, Ghent
www.marijncoertjens.be
Mouthwatering pâtisseries, tarts and gingerbread.

3 Neuhaus
www.neuhauschocolates.com
Credited with inventing the praline and the *ballotin* (box).

4 Dumon
www.chocolatierdumon.be
Excellent chocolatier originating from Torhout, near Bruges: a cut above the mass-market producers.

5 Wittamer
www.wittamer.com
Chocolates, gateaux, macaroons and biscuits to die for (see p78).

6 Pierre Marcolini
www.eu.marcolini.com
Fabulous chocolates made entirely from raw ingredients.

7 Mary
www.mary.be
Chocolates of exquisite quality.

8 Galler
A mass-market but high-standard manufacturer. Its famous *Langues de Chat* (cat's tongues) are shaped in a jokey cat's face.

9 Maison Dandoy
Supreme biscuit manufacturer, famed for their *speculoos* (see p78).

10 Jules Destrooper
www.jules-destrooper.com
Manufacturer of biscuits since 1886. Its blue-and-white boxes contain waffles, florentines and almond thins.

🔟 Brussels, Bruges, Antwerp & Ghent for Free

1 Grand Place, Brussels
The spectacular centrepiece of Brussels is a marvel of ornate architecture. There are a couple of attractions with entrance charges to visit here, but the best is free: standing in the middle looking at the façades in wonder *(see pp14–15)*.

2 Manneken-Pis, Brussels
On view in all his unashamed glory, just a short walk from the Grand Place, is Brussels' most famous and notorious mascot *(see p73)*. Access to the statue is free, but you will have to pay to see his collection of costumes at the Maison du Roi *(see p15)*, unless you go on the first Sunday of the month.

3 Africa Museum
The Africa Museum *(see p86)* in Tervuren features occasional pop-up exhibitions that are free on the weekends. The museum also has beautifully landscaped gardens that are free of charge. You can saunter past monumental geometric topiary and stunning Neo-Classical fountains, picnic near the neatly laid out lakes and stroll through ancient woodland.

4 The European Parliament and the Parlementarium, Brussels
For all avid political enthusiasts, here's a chance to see what goes on at the EU Parliament and get an insight into the lives and work of MEPs – and all for free *(see p84)*.

The Maagdenhuismuseum, Antwerp

5 Museums: free entry days
Many of the publicly owned museums offer free entry one day a month. For example, on the first Wednesday each month, after 1pm, there is no charge at the Musées Royaux des Beaux-Arts *(see pp18–19)* and the Musée des Instruments de Musique *(see pp20–21)* in Brussels. Most public museums in Antwerp are also free on the first Wednesday of the month; the Maagdenhuismuseum *(see p104)* and the MAS *(see p102)* on the last.

6 Graslei and Korenlei, Ghent
These two historic quays, facing each other over the River Leie, are joined by a bridge, the Sint-Michielsbrug. This provides an excellent viewpoint, taking in both quays and the towers of the Sint-Niklaaskerk, the Belfort and Sint-Baafskathedraal *(see p109)*.

Graslei Quay, Ghent

7 Walking in Bruges

One of the best things to do in Bruges is simply to walk. Bring stout shoes (for the cobbles) and wander. Virtually every sector of the city within the ovoid perimeter – formed by canals and roads that track the path of the old city walls – yields something of interest. Many hotels will supply maps with walks marked on them.

8 Centraal Station, Antwerp

MAP V2

This is a classic monument to the golden age of railways: a station of palatial richness, referencing just about every architectural style, and glittering with gilded ornamentation, polished marble and glass. Built in 1905, it was the culminating master-work of the Bruges architect Louis Delacenserie (1838–1909).

Palais de Justice, Brussels

9 Palais de Justice, Brussels

This colossal pile, which dominates the city skyline, still serves as a law court, so it's normally possible to enter during working hours on weekdays. It was the biggest building in Europe when com-pleted in 1883 after 17 years of construction, and the interior is as vast and elaborate as the exterior (see p76).

10 Churches

Many of the churches are free to enter (although you are invited to leave a donation). There are excep-tions, such as Antwerp Cathedral.

TOP 10 BUDGET TIPS

Centraal station, Antwerp

1 Belgian railways offer numerous discounts, eg for weekend travel, the over 65s, under 12s. Visit www.belgianrail.be.

2 Hotel prices fluctuate according to business travel patterns and tourist flow. Brussels offers competitive rates at week-ends, and reduced prices in August; in Bruges, weekdays off-season are cheaper.

3 Check if breakfast is included in your hotel price. If not, breakfast in the hotel will add €10–25 per person per night to your stay.

4 Car parking is most expensive in city centres, and much cheaper – free, even – on the outskirts. Park and walk to Bruges, Antwerp or Ghent, or take the park and ride to Brussels.

5 A 24/48/72-hour pass or preloadable multi-journey MOBIB Basic card can save money on public transport. This is particularly relevant in Brussels, where you may wish to travel to the museums and sights of Outer Brussels, beyond normal walking distance.

6 Museum passes allow you to visit several museums in a given city for a single, reduced price.

7 In restaurants, fixed-price set-menus, particularly at lunchtime, can be real bargains.

8 Belgium is famous for its *frites* (chips), and a good chip stall (*friterie/ frietkot*) can provide a cheap meal.

9 Picnics are a great way to save money. Delicatessens, bread shops and pâtisseries offer great prepared food – sandwiches, flans, tarts, tubs of salad.

10 Visitors from outside the EU can reclaim most sales tax (TVA/BWT) on purchases above a minimum value of €125 from any one shop. Visit www.brusselsairport.be.

Festivals and Events

Exhibit at Gentse Floraliën, Ghent

Gentse Floraliën, Ghent

Late Apr (next in 2027)

This flower show is held once every five years, with floral displays throughout the city centre and at the main Flanders Expo halls. Ghent's flower-growing industry is famous above all for its begonias, azaleas, rhododendrons and roses.

Heilig Bloedprocessie, Bruges

Ascension Day (May)

Bruges' biggest day out, the Procession of the Holy Blood follows an 800-year-old tradition: 40 days after Easter, the sacred relic of the Holy Blood is paraded around the streets in a colourful, spectacular, but at heart solemn procession featuring sumptuous medieval and biblical costumes.

Festival van Vlaanderen

Dates are mainly Jun–Oct
■ www.festival.be

An impressive programme of classical music – as well as jazz, world music and dance – takes place across Flanders every summer and autumn, with performances in the main venues, as well as in churches and other historic buildings.

Ommegang, Brussels

Two days in late Jun/early Jul

In Brussels' most spectacular parade, some 2,000 participants, dressed as Renaissance nobles, guildsmen, mounted soldiers and entertainers, perform an *ommegang* (tour) in the Grand Place. Running since 1549, this tradition honours the coming of Charles V to Brussels.

Foire du Midi, Brussels

Mid-Jul–mid-Aug

This big, rollicking, noisy late-summer fun fair set out along the Boulevard du Midi has the newest rides plus dodgems, roller coasters and all the other old favourites.

6 Planten van de Meiboom, Brussels

9 Aug (1:30pm onwards)

This jolly slice of ancient folklore dates back to 1213. Led by the Confrérie des Compagnons de Saint-Laurent, dressed in wacky costumes, and accompanied by seven traditional giant figures, the participants parade a may tree around central Brussels, before planting it on the corner of Rue du Marais and Rue des Sables.

Brass section of an orchestra performing at the Festival van Vlaanderen

7 Reiefeest, Bruges
Last 10 days of Aug (next in 2023)

This festival, held every five years, celebrates the River Reie's role in the city's history. A series of historical scenes is performed at night beside the water, creating a magical effect and bringing the city's architecture to life.

8 Praalstoet van de Gouden Boom, Bruges
Late Aug (next in 2024)

First performed in 1958, the Pageant of the Golden Tree takes place in Bruges every five years or so. In a vast costumed parade, the people of the city evoke the glory days of the Burgundian era.

9 Toussaint, throughout Belgium
1–2 Nov

All Saints' Day is followed by the Jour des Morts, the Day of the Dead – time when Belgians honour their departed by tidying up the graveyards and laying flowers – mainly chrysanthemums.

Celebrating Fête de Saint-Nicolas

10 Fête de Saint-Nicolas, throughout Belgium
6 Dec

The Feast of St Nicholas (Sinterklaas in Dutch) is celebrated by children with more enthusiasm than Christmas. St Nicholas (the original Santa Claus), dressed as the Bishop of Myra, walks the streets with his sidekick Zwarte Piet. Children receive presents, sweets and *speculoos* biscuits.

TOP 10 SPECTATOR SPORTS AND VENUES

1 Ronde van Vlaanderen
First Sun in Apr
Classic of the cycling calendar.

2 Liège-Bastogne-Liège
Third Sun in Apr
Oldest cycling classic in the World Tour.

3 Zesdaagse van Vlaanderen-Gent
MAP P6 ■ Late Nov ■ 't Kuipke, Citadelpark
One of the most important meetings for European speed cycling.

4 Jan Breydel Stadium (Olympiapark)
Olympialaan 74, 8200 (Sint-Andries) ■ 050 40 21 35 ■ www.clubbrugge.be
Stadium shared by Club Brugge and Cercle Brugge.

5 20 km of Brussels
Last Sun in May
Brussels' mini-marathon.

6 Belgian Grand Prix
Spa-Francorchamps ■ Late Aug
A must for all committed petrol-heads.

7 Hippodrome Wellington, Ostend
Horseracing every Monday in July and August (harness and flatracing).

8 King Baudouin Stadium
MAP F1 ■ Ave du Marathon 135, 1020 BRU (Laeken) ■ 02 474 39 40
Athletics, cycle meetings and international soccer matches.

9 Constant Vanden Stock Stadium
MAP F2 ■ Avenue Théo Verbeeck, 1070 BRU (Anderlecht) ■ 02 895 08 04 (for football tickets) ■ www.rsca.be
The home ground of RSC Anderlecht.

10 Memorial Van Damme
MAP F1 ■ Sep ■ Stade Roi Baudouin
Important athletics meeting.

Athletes at Memorial Van Damme

🔟 Excursions

The stunning town hall, Leuven

1 Leuven
Tourist Office: Naamsestraat 3 ▪ 016 20 30 20 ▪ www.visitleuven.be

The old university town of Leuven (French: Louvain) has a deep charm, derived from its compact human scale and many historic buildings – chief among them the Stadhuis, the most beautiful Gothic town hall of them all with its lace-like detail.

2 Walibi Belgium
Belgium's biggest and best-known theme park – a good day out for the kids *(see p57)*.

3 Forêt de Soignes
Drève du Rouge-Cloître 4, 1160 Auderghem ▪ www.foret-de-soignes.be

The magnificent ancient beech forests of Soignes offer a splendid landscape for walking or cycling – particularly in autumn, when the beech trees turn golden. There are two arboretums, at Groenendaal and Tervuren, and an information centre on the site of the 14th-century Abbaye du Rouge-Cloître.

4 Namur
Tourist Office: Place de la Station ▪ 081 24 64 49 ▪ www.namurtourisme.be

An attractive town on the confluence of the Meuse and Sambre rivers, Namur is known for its mighty Citadelle perched dramatically on a steep-sided hill.

5 Mechelen
Tourist Office: Vleeshouwers-straat 6 ▪ 015 29 76 54 ▪ www.visit.mechelen.be

Mechelen (French: Malines) was a trading city in the Burgundian era, and centre of power under Margaret of Austria (1507–15; 1519–30). Dominating the city is the vast bell-tower of Sint-Romboutskathedraal.

6 Lier
Tourist Office: Grote Markt 58 ▪ 038 00 05 55 ▪ www.visitlier.be

This charming town to the southeast of Antwerp has a handsome collection of historic buildings clustered around the Grote Markt, and a 13th-century *beguinage* listed as a UNESCO World

Charming buildings line the water at Lier

Heritage Site, but its most famous possession is the Zimmertoren, a 14th-century watchtower with a Centenary Clock.

Butte de Lion mound, Waterloo

7 Waterloo
Route du Lion 1815, 1420 Braine-l'Alleud ■ 023 85 19 12 ■ Open 10am–6:30pm daily (till 7pm Jul & Aug); Nov–Mar: 10am–5:30pm daily ■ Adm ■ www.waterloo1815.be

It was near Waterloo, 15 km (9 miles) south of Brussels, that Napoleon was finally defeated. The battlefield has been a tourist site since the battle itself. The 1815 Memorial visitor centre is a good place to start.

8 Oostende
Tourist Office: Monacoplein 2 ■ 059 70 11 99 ■ www.visitoostende.be

Oostende is famous as a coastal resort and for its excellent seafood.

It also has surprisingly good collections of art in the Mu.ZEE, featuring local artist James Ensor and the Symbolists.

9 Damme
Tourist Office: Jacob van Maerlantstraat 3 ■ 050 28 86 10 ■ www.visitdamme.be

A pretty cluster of late-medieval buildings is all that remains of the once-prosperous town at the head of the canal to Bruges. A pleasant excursion by boat, bus or bicycle.

10 Ieper (Ypres)
In Flanders Fields: Lakenhallen, Grote Markt 34 ■ 057 23 92 20 ■ Open Apr–mid-Nov: 10am–6pm daily; mid-Nov–Mar: 10am–5pm Tue–Sun; closed 3 weeks in Jan, some public hols ■ Adm ■ www.inflandersfields.be ■ www.toerisme-ieper.be

Ieper (French: Ypres) was one of the great medieval trading cities of Flanders. Its historic past was all but erased when it became the focus of bitter trench warfare in World War I. Today, it is a centre for visits to the trenches and the cemeteries, and site of the Menin Gate, the memorial arch marking the road along which soldiers marched. But the real draw is In Flanders Fields, a museum depicting the background of the war, its experiences and horrors – a richly informative and moving experience.

Brussels, Bruges, Antwerp & Ghent
Area by Area

Steenhouwersdijk, one of the most pictureque
stretches of the canal, Bruges

🔟 Central Brussels

Central Brussels is contained within a clearly defined shape called the Pentagon. Nowadays this outline is formed by a ring road called the Petite Ceinture, which follows the path of the old city walls. Little remains of the walls, but one old city gate, the Porte de Hal, still stands, and gives an indication of just how massive the fortifications were. Most of historic Brussels is within these bounds, including both the commercial and popular districts of the Lower Town, and the aristocratic quarter of the Upper Town, which includes the Royal Palace. As well as cultural gems, you will find places to stay and eat, good shops, and vibrant cafés and bars.

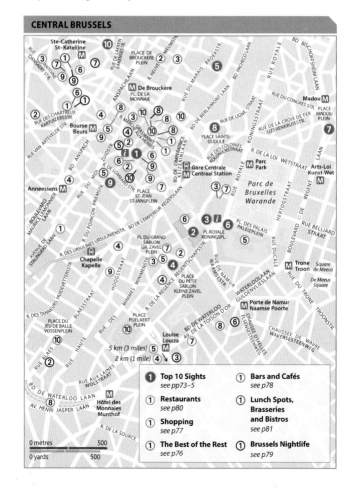

CENTRAL BRUSSELS

① **Top 10 Sights** see pp73–5	① **Bars and Cafés** see p78
① **Restaurants** see p80	① **Lunch Spots, Brasseries and Bistros** see p81
① **Shopping** see p77	
① **The Best of the Rest** see p76	① **Brussels Nightlife** see p79

0 metres 500
0 yards 500

The impressive Grand Place during the Tapis des Fleurs flower festival

1 The Grand Place

No trip to Brussels would be complete without a visit to the Grand Place – even if it's just to stock up on some Belgian biscuits or chocolates. A remarkable legacy of the city's Gothic and Renaissance past, it is also a monument to the values and ingenuity of the artisans and merchants who were the architects of Brussels' prosperity (see pp14–15).

The Card Players by De Braekeleer, Musées Royaux des Beaux-Arts

2 Musées Royaux des Beaux-Arts

The premier art gallery of Belgium focuses almost exclusively on Flemish and Belgian art, and is more rewarding for it. Highlights include rare works by Pieter Bruegel the Elder and the exhilarating Rubens collection. It is interlinked with the Fin-de-Siècle Museum and the Magritte Museum (see pp18–19).

3 Musée des Instruments de Musique

The famous "mim" collection of historical and contemporary musical instruments is housed in the remarkable Art Nouveau department store known as "Old England". A visitor guidance system brings the exhibits to life (see pp20–21).

4 Sablon

MAP C4 ■ Rue de la Régence 3B ■ Church: open 9am–6:30pm Mon–Fri, 10am–7pm Sat–Sun

The name Sablon refers to the sandy marshland that occupied this site until the 17th century. The Place du Grand Sablon is a centre for antiques and is home to leading chocolate makers: Pierre Marcolini and Wittamer. The Place du Petit Sablon park is adorned with statues of the medieval guilds of Brussels. Separating the two is the Église Notre-Dame du Sablon (see p46).

Église Notre-Dame du Sablon

A visitor browses comic designs at the Comics Art Museum

⑤ Comics Art Museum

Reflecting the huge popularity of comic-strip books in Belgium – and, indeed, most of continental Europe – this unique museum, formerly known as the Centre Belge de la Bande Dessinée, is a shrine to the art form. Archive material and other exhibits focus above all on Belgian contributors to the genre – most notably, of course, on Hergé, the creator of Tintin (see pp26–7).

Underground at Palais Coudenberg

⑥ Palais Coudenberg

MAP D4 ■ Place des Palais 7 ■ 02 500 45 54 ■ Open 9:30am–5pm Tue–Fri, 10am–6pm Sat & Sun; 10am–6pm daily Jul & Aug ■ Adm

Accessed via the BELvue Museum (see p76), this archaeological site was once the medieval Coudenberg Palace that stood on Place Royale. The palace was the home of various rulers, including Holy Roman Emperor Charles V, for more than 600 years until it burned down in 1731. The highlight is the impressive Aula Magna banqueting hall, which was the scene of Charles V's abdication in 1555.

⑦ Musée Charlier

MAP E3 ■ Avenue des Arts 16, 1210 Saint Josse-ten-Noorde ■ 02 220 26 91 ■ Open noon–5pm Mon–Thu, 10am–1pm Fri ■ Adm ■ www.charlier museum.be

Brussels is a city of grand old 19th-century mansions, or *maisons de maître*. This museum provides a rare opportunity to see inside one. The original owner, Henri van Curtsem, commissioned Victor Horta (see p23) to redesign the interior. In the hands of van Curtsem's adoptive heir, sculptor Guillaume Charlier, the mansion became a centre for Brussels' avant-garde. On his death in 1925, Charlier left the house to the city, and it retains much of the decor of his era. There are works displayed by leading artists of the time, such as James Ensor, Léon Frédéric, Fernand Khnopff and Rik Wouters, plus an impressive collection of antique furniture.

⑧ Cathédrale des Saints Michel et Gudule

MAP D3 ■ Parvis Sainte-Gudule ■ 02 217 83 45 ■ Open 8am–6pm daily ■ Adm only for Museum of Church Treasures and Crypt

Brussels' largest and finest church was built from 1226 onwards and showcases over 300 years' worth of architectural design. Highlights inside include an enormous Baroque oak pulpit, splendid Renaissance stained-glass windows, and access to the treasury and preserved remnants of the old Romanesque

THE PENTAGON

The first city walls to enclose Brussels were built in about 1100 but the city expanded and they were superseded in 1381, creating the neat pentagon shape that is evident today. The walls were replaced in the mid-19th century by tree-lined boulevards, but the ramparts of the Porte de Hal *(see p76)* still offer panoramic city views.

church that once stood here. Dedicated to St Michael, patron saint of the city, the cathedral also acknowledges in its name St Gudule, a local 8th-century saint who outfoxed the Devil. The cathedral is often used for royal weddings and state funerals.

⑨ Manneken-Pis

In Brussels you can't avoid this cheeky chap, famously relieving himself with carefree abandon, just as little boys do. Among other things, he's on postcards, T-shirts, key rings and corkscrews. So why not take a pilgrimage to see the real thing – a tiny bronze statue – and bask in the happy absurdity of it all? It must be worth a photograph *(see p16)*.

⑩ Église St-Jean-Baptiste au Béguinage

MAP B1 ■ Place du Béguinage
■ 02 217 87 42 ■ Open 11am–5pm
Tue–Sat, 2–5pm Sun

Considered to be one of the country's prettiest churches, this Baroque beauty belonged to a *béguinage* *(see p92)* and dates from the 17th century.

Église St-Jean-Baptiste

Église Sainte-Catherine
Cathédrale des Saints Michel et Gudule
Rue Dansaert
Bourse
Parc de Bruxelles
Grand Place
Dandoy
Manneken-Pis
Musée des Instruments de Musique
Musées Royaux des Beaux-Arts
Palais Royal
Sablon district
Rue de la Régence

▶ MORNING

Start off with the essentials: a stroll around the **Grand Place** *(see pp14–15)* and a trip to the **Manneken-Pis** *(see p16)*, stopping for a waffle at the **Dandoy** shop *(see p63)* at Rue Charles Buls 14. Now head back to the Bourse *(see p16)*, and go west along Rue Dansaert, the street for cutting-edge fashion. Turn right at the Rue du Vieux Marché aux Grains and walk up to the **Église Sainte-Catherine,** a church designed in 1854 by Joseph Poelaert, also responsible for the Palais de Justice. It stands on reclaimed land at the head of a canal now covered over by the Place Sainte-Catherine. This was the site of the old fish market, and is still famous for its fish restaurants – an ideal place to stop for lunch.

AFTERNOON

Walk back east, stopping at the **Cathédrale des Saints Michel et Gudule** *(see p74)* before heading up the hill to Rue Royale. Take a stroll in the pleasant **Parc de Bruxelles**, then walk south to the **Palais Royal** *(see p76)* and the elegant 17th-century Place Royale, with its statue of the 11th-century crusader Godefroy de Bouillon. You're now a stone's throw from both the **Musées Royaux des Beaux-Arts** *(see pp18–19)* and the **Musée des Instruments de Musique** *(see pp20–21)*. For refreshments, continue down the Rue de la Régence to the cafés and chocolate shops of ⬤ **Sablon** *(see p73)*.

See map on p72 ←

The Best of the Rest

1 Galeries Royales Saint-Hubert

When it opened in 1847, this very elegant shopping arcade was the first and grandest in Europe (see p16).

2 Musée du Costume et de la Dentelle

On display are exquisite examples of costume and lace, an industry that employed 10,000 women in mid-19th-century Brussels (see p16).

3 Place des Martyrs
MAP C2

The 445 "martyrs" killed in the Belgian Revolution of 1830 were laid to rest in a crypt beneath this square.

4 Église Notre-Dame de la Chapelle

MAP B4 ▪ Place de la Chapelle ▪ Open Jun–Sep: 9am–7pm daily, Oct–Mar: 9am–6pm daily

This large, atmospheric church is like something out of a Bruegel painting – aptly so, since Pieter Bruegel the Elder is buried here.

5 Palais Royal and BELvue Museum

MAP D4 ▪ Place des Palais. Palais Royal: 02 551 20 20; Open Jul–mid-Sep: 10:30am–5pm Tue–Sun ▪ BELvue Museum: 02 500 45 54; Open 10am–5pm Tue–Fri (Jul & Aug, weekends: till 6pm) ▪ Adm

See how the other half lived in the grand rooms of the Royal Palace. A former hotel next to the palace houses a museum devoted to the history of Belgium since 1830.

6 Palais de Charles de Lorraine

MAP C4 ▪ Place du Musée 1 ▪ Opening times vary; check website for details ▪ Adm ▪ www.kbr.be

This delightful 18th-century palace, containing the Royal Library of Belgium, hosts temporary exhibitions.

7 Cinematek

MAP D4 ▪ Rue Baron Horta 9 ▪ 02 551 19 00 ▪ Open daily ▪ Adm ▪ www.cinematek.be

A bijou cinema with a fascinating collection in the foyer that traces the early history of the moving image.

8 Porte de Hal

MAP B6 ▪ Boulevard du Midi 150 ▪ 02 534 34 50 ▪ Open 9:30am–5pm Mon–Thu, 10am–5pm Sat & Sun ▪ Adm (free from 1pm first Wed of month)

The sole surviving gate of the 14th-century city walls houses a museum of defences and history.

9 Illusion Brussels

MAP C3 ▪ 22 Rue du Marché aux Fromages, 1000 Bru ▪ 02 828 16 00 ▪ Open 10am–7pm Mon–Thu, 9am–9pm Fri–Sun (last adm 45 min before closing) ▪ Adm

This special-effects museum will appeal to both children and adults.

10 Palais de Justice

MAP B5 ▪ Place Poelaert

The glorious Neo-Classical building is one of the largest courthouses in the world.

Entrance of the Palais de Justice

Shopping

1 Galeries Royales Saint-Hubert

Home to luxury shops including jewellers and crystal makers *(see p16)*.

2 Rue Neuve
MAP C2

This pedestrianized shopping street close to the city centre features many of the main European fashion chains and a large Inno department store at the northern end.

3 Rue Antoine Dansaert
MAP A2

Many of Antwerp's designers are represented in the shops along this eclectic shopping street, and there are several outlets for notable Belgian fashion labels, too.

Christmas market stall

4 Christmas Market
MAP B3

From early December to early January, this market offers all things Christmassy – crafts, decorations, gifts – in the streets around the Bourse and on Quai aux Briques.

5 Place du Grand Sablon
MAP C4

There are antiques shops fronting the square, but poke around in some of the side passages as well. Two of the finest chocolatiers, Wittamer and Pierre Marcolini, are here *(see p63)*.

6 Galerie Agora
MAP C3 ▪ Rue du Marché aux Herbes

This maze-like covered arcade sells inexpensive T-shirts, leather goods, costume jewellery and incense.

Second-hand books, Galerie Bortier

7 Galerie Bortier
MAP C3 ▪ Rue de la Madeleine 55 ▪ Closed Sun, Mon

Smaller than the Galeries Royales Saint-Hubert, but just as elegant. Here you'll find second-hand books, prints, postcards and posters.

8 Avenue Louise and Galerie de la Toison d'Or
MAP C6/D5

Top-name international couturiers, including Chanel and Hermès, can be found along Avenue Louise and the adjoining Boulevard de Waterloo. The covered Galerie de la Toison d'Or, a little further to the east, is also a major shopping hub.

9 Around the Grand Place
MAP B3/C3

Rue du Marché aux Herbes, Rue du Marché au Charbon and Rue du Midi are good for independent boutiques, jewellers, bookshops and food shops.

10 Rue Blaes and Place du Jeu de Balle
MAP B5

Place du Jeu de Balle has a daily flea market (6am–2pm) selling antiques, junk and curios, and there are similar shops along Rue Blaes.

See map on p72

Bars and Cafés

① Le Greenwich
MAP B2 ▪ Rue des Chartreux 7

An established Brussels favourite, especially popular with an avid chess-playing crowd. It was a former hangout of Magritte.

A game of chess at Le Greenwich

② Le Roy d'Espagne
MAP C3 ▪ Grand Place 1

A famous watering-hole in the old bakers' guildhouse. There is a medieval air to the interior decor. Also serves light meals.

③ Au Bon Vieux Temps
MAP C3 ▪ Impasse St- Nicolas 4

Blink and you'll miss this traditional 17th-century tavern tucked down a side street off Rue du Marché aux Herbes. This is a great spot for escaping the bustle outside.

④ Moeder Lambic
MAP B3 ▪ Place Fontainas 8

The central Brussels branch of the revered Saint-Gilles "beer academy", this splendid bar offers hundreds of mainly Belgian beers, dozens of them on tap, and all are listed in the catalogue. If you can't decide which, ask the staff: they are experts and always happy to help.

⑤ Le Cirio
MAP B3 ▪ Rue de la Bourse 18

Another classic, Le Cirio has been open since 1886 and is famous for its *half-en-half* – a mix of still and sparkling white wine.

⑥ Maison Dandoy
MAP C3 ▪ Rue Charles Buls 14

This artisanal bakery offers delicious handmade *speculoos* (Belgian spiced biscuits) and waffles topped with chocolate sauce, or fruit and whipped cream.

⑦ Wittamer
MAP C4 ▪ Place du Grand Sablon 12–13

The world-class chocolatier has a seating area under a bright pink canopy where you can sample its heavenly products with a cup of tea or coffee on the side. The praline is particularly popular with visitors.

⑧ Peck 47
MAP B2 ▪ Rue du Marché aux Poulets 47

Visit this popular café serving all-day brunch, snacks, coffee and cakes. Vegan and gluten-free options are available too.

⑨ Bonnefooi
MAP B3 ▪ Rue des Pierres 8

This lively bar draws a young crowd with its live music on week nights and DJs at the weekend. Great atmosphere especially in summer.

⑩ À La Mort Subite
MAP C2 ▪ Rue Montagne aux Herbes Potagères 7

"Sudden Death" may sound rather alarming, but this famous bar, redesigned in Rococo style in 1926, is named after a card game.

À La Mort Subite

Brussels Nightlife

Archiduc in full swing

selection, which includes a number of brews from the nearby En Stoemelings microbrewery.

⑤ The Music Village
MAP B3 ▪ Rue des Pierres 50
▪ www.themusicvillage.com
Jazz and blues bar with live concerts taking place every night: 8:30pm on weeknights; 9pm on weekends. Dinner is available either before or during the performances.

⑥ Spirito Brussels
MAP C6 ▪ Rue Stassart 18
▪ 483 580 697
Housed in a former Anglican church, this swish nightclub/restaurant features gold and crystal decor, beautiful lighting and a big dancefloor.

⑦ Madame Moustache
MAP B2 ▪ 5–7 Quai au Bois à Brûler ▪ 0489 739 912
A retro club (1950s–80s) and concert venue, featuring rock'n'roll, swing, funk and jazz. It prides itself on its quirky cabaret atmosphere.

⑧ Delirium Village
MAP C3 ▪ Impasse de la Fidélité 4 ▪ 02 514 44 34
This lively pub complex holds the Guinness World Record for the most beers available for tasting (over 2,000), including a variety of local craft beers.

⑨ Café Roskam
MAP B2 ▪ Rue de Flandre 9
▪ www.café-roskam.be
With a friendly local vibe, this lively central late-night bar turns into a first-rate jazz club on Sunday evenings.

⑩ The Green Man
MAP C3 ▪ Rue des Chapeliers 26
▪ 0473 405 399 ▪ Closed Mon–Wed
A cosy cocktail bar offering outdoor seating for balmy evenings. The knowledgeable bar staff can concoct sophisticated cocktails. Live music on most weekends.

① Archiduc
MAP B2 ▪ Rue Antoine Dansaert 6–8 ▪ 02 512 06 52
This legendary 1930s Art Deco bar – designed like a cruise liner – has entertained all the jazz greats. The place picks up after midnight.

② Fuse
MAP B5 ▪ Rue Blaes 208
▪ 02 511 97 89
Behind the gritty industrial exterior lies the best club in town. World-class DJs spin a mix of techno and drum 'n' bass.

③ Bloody Louis
MAP C6 ▪ Avenue Louise 32
▪ www.bloodylouis.be
Big, brash and resolutely electro, this club situated in the Louise Gallery attracts big name DJs.

④ La Reserve
MAP C3 ▪ Petite Rue au Beurre 2a ▪ 02 511 60 06
La Reserve is the oldest LGBTQ+ bar in town. It attracts locals and tourists alike for its lively weekend atmosphere and excellent beer

See map on p72

Restaurants

1 Comme Chez Soi
MAP B4 ▪ Place Rouppe 23
▪ 02 512 29 21 ▪ Closed Sun–Tue
▪ €€€

Brussels' most celebrated restaurant is family-run and has two Michelin stars. For a taste of the superlative, innovative French cuisine, be sure to book weeks ahead.

Interiors of L'Ecailler du Palais Royal

2 L'Ecailler du Palais Royal
MAP C4 ▪ Rue Bodenbroek 18 ▪ 02 512 87 51 ▪ Closed mid-Jul–mid-Aug ▪ €€€

One of Brussels' most prestigious fish restaurants, this quiet, refined establishment attracts a mature clientele with its classic cuisine.

3 Au Vieux Saint Martin
MAP C4 ▪ Place du Grand Sablon 38 ▪ 02 512 64 76 ▪ €€

Tuck into seasonal Belgian cuisine while admiring the Modern art on the walls of this restaurant.

4 Isabelle Arpin
MAP G2 ▪ Avenue Louise 362
▪ 0492 971 927 ▪ Closed Mon, Thu–Fri, Sat D ▪ €€€

Each dish at this spot is a veritable work of art and a subtle balance of flavours, colours and textures.

5 La Villa Lorraine
MAP G2 ▪ Avenue du Vivier d'Oie 75 ▪ 02 374 31 63 ▪ Closed Sun, Mon ▪ €€€

Try creative cuisine here by renowned Belgian chef Yves Mattagne. There's also a lounge and a cocktail bar.

6 La Belle Maraîchère
MAP B2 ▪ Place Sainte-Catherine 11a ▪ 02 512 97 59
▪ Closed Wed, Thu ▪ €€€

A favourite with locals for decades, this timeless wood-panelled restaurant serves top-rate fish dishes.

7 Cospaia
MAP C5 ▪ Rue Crespel 1
▪ 02 513 03 03 ▪ Closed L, Sun ▪ €€

Located on the southern edge of the Pentagon, this sleek restaurant and cocktail bar serves classic cuisine prepared with fresh produce. It features two elegant dining rooms, a terrace and a rooftop.

8 Restaurant Vincent
MAP C3 ▪ Rue des Dominicains 8–10 ▪ 02 511 26 07 ▪ Closed Sun
▪ €€€

Dine on mussels and flambéed steaks in a room decorated with old, tiled marine murals.

9 La Bonne Chère
MAP B4 ▪ Rue Notre-Seigneur 19 ▪ 02 523 75 55 ▪ Closed Sun, Mon & Sat L ▪ €€

Enjoy seasonal bistro-style cuisine in this rustic yet elegant restaurant.

10 Aux Armes de Bruxelles
MAP C3 ▪ Rue des Bouchers 13
▪ 02 511 55 50 ▪ €€

Founded in 1921, Aux Armes de Bruxelles is an institution, praised for its white-linen elegance and impeccable Belgian cooking.

Exterior of Aux Armes de Bruxelles

Lunch Spots, Brasseries and Bistros

1 O la Vache
MAP B2 ▪ Rue de Flandre 25 ▪ 0487 903 480 ▪ Closed Mon ▪ €

Expect mouthwatering grilled meats cooked over a charcoal grill in an open kitchen at this candlelit bistro.

2 In 't Spinnekopke
MAP A3 ▪ Place du Jardin-aux-Fleurs 1 ▪ 02 512 92 05 ▪ Closed Sun, Mon ▪ €€

An appealing *estaminet* (traditional pub) that stands by its 18th-century heritage to present a menu of fine Belgian-Bruxellois dishes.

3 Bozar Restaurant
MAP D3 ▪ Rue Baron Horta 3 ▪ 02 503 00 00 ▪ Closed Sun, Mon, Tue & Sat L ▪ €€€

Designed by Victor Horta in 1928, this Michelin-starred restaurant is an Art Deco gem that has been revamped after its renovation. The lauded chef prepares faultless Belgian cuisine.

4 Les Petits Oignons
MAP C5 ▪ Rue de la Régence 25 ▪ 02 511 76 15 ▪ €€

This brasserie offers Mediterranean and French cuisine. It is known for its carefully selected wine list.

5 Nüetnigenough
MAP B3 ▪ Rue du Lombard 25 ▪ 02 513 78 84 ▪ Closed Mon–Fri L ▪ €

Featuring Belgian specialities, this lively bistro also offers a beer menu.

6 Le Pain Quotidien
MAP B2 ▪ Rue Antoine Dansaert 16a ▪ 02 502 23 61 ▪ €

Selling excellent bread with delicious fillings, as well as tempting pastries, Le Pain Quotidien ("Daily Bread") is a huge success. This is the original and most central branch in the city.

7 Le Pré Salé
MAP B2 ▪ Rue de Flandre 20 ▪ 02 513 65 45 ▪ €€

This bistro offers delicious Belgian classics such as green eels, *stoemp (see p61)* and *moules marinière* (mussels in white wine), all served with chips and homemade mayonnaise. The set lunch menu is good value.

Art Deco style Taverne du Passage

8 Taverne du Passage
MAP C3 ▪ Galerie de la Reine 30 ▪ 02 512 14 13 ▪ €€

A traditional 1930s Belgian diner with accomplished waiters and an enthusiastic local clientele. The fish dishes are excellent.

9 't Kelderke
MAP C3 ▪ Grand Place 15 ▪ 02 513 73 44 ▪ €€

This 17th-century cellar-restaurant delivers feasts of Belgian cuisine. The good food attracts appreciative locals as well as tourists.

10 Chez Léon
MAP C3 ▪ Rue des Bouchers 18 ▪ 02 511 14 15 ▪ €

Established in 1893, this restaurant is a *moules-frites* specialist that has become an international brand.

See map on p72

TOP 10 Outer Brussels

Parc du Cinquantenaire

Over the centuries, Brussels expanded beyond the old city walls, absorbing surrounding towns and villages. These outlying communes such as Ixelles, Saint-Gilles and Anderlecht still retain their distinctive characters, resulting in a huge variety across outer Brussels. An excellent public transport system makes it easy to get around these suburbs, and the highlights listed here are worth the journey.

1 Art and Design Atomium Museum

MAP F1 ▪ Place de Belgique, 1020 BRU (Laeken) ▪ 02 669 49 29 ▪ Open 11am–7pm daily ▪ Adm ▪ www.designmuseum.brussels

In the shadow of the Atomium, this museum focuses solely on modern design. The main highlight is the huge Plasticarium collection of the largest plastic design objects in Europe, from playful Pop Art to the iconic Post-Modern cantilever chair. The temporary exhibitions focus on the design world, projected through various themes and materials.

OUTER BRUSSELS

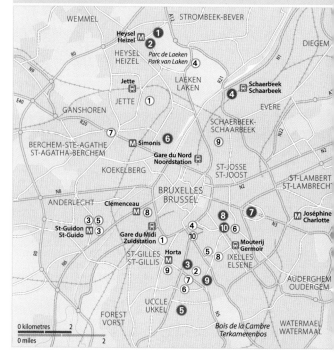

③ Horta Museum
A symphony in Art Nouveau design (see pp22–3).

④ Train World
MAP G2 ■ Place Princesse Élisabeth 5, 1030 BRU (Schaerbeek) ■ 02 224 74 98 ■ Open 10am–5pm Tue–Sun (last entry 3:30pm); closed public hols ■ Adm ■ www.train world.be

Opened in 2015, this railway museum displays the impressive historic collection of Belgian national railways (NMBS/SNCB). It contains locomotives dating back to the 1840s, plus carriages and all sorts of railway paraphernalia, theatrically presented with dramatic lighting, sound effects and imaginative props that help to personalize the exhibits. The beautiful and immaculately restored 19th-century Schaerbeek station is the main hub (accessible by train, tram and bus), with adjacent modern, purpose-built exhibition halls housing the main exhibits.

The Atomium

② The Atomium
MAP F1 (inset) ■ Square de l'Atomium, 1020 BRU (Laeken) ■ 02 475 47 75 ■ Open 10am–6pm daily ■ Adm ■ www.atomium.be

This giant model of an iron crystal was built as Belgium's exhibit at Brussels' 1958 Universal Exposition. It stands 102 m (335 ft) tall and has nine 18 m (59 ft) diameter spheres.

Van Buuren Museum

⑤ Van Buuren Museum
MAP G3 ■ Ave Léo Errera 41, 1180 BRU (Uccle) ■ 02 343 48 51 ■ Museum & garden: open 2–5:30pm Wed–Mon ■ Adm ■ www.museum vanbuuren.be

This beautifully preserved Art Deco home of David and Alice van Buuren has excellent furniture and stained glass, plus contemporary paintings.

6 Pixel Museum

MAP G2 ■ Tour et Taxis, Av du Port 86c, 1000 BRU ■ Open 10am–6pm Wed–Sun ■ Adm €12 (€9 for 3–18 yrs), €10 seniors, €35 family (admits 4), free for under 3s ■ www.pixel-museum.brussels

This museum dedicated to video games and video game art is a must for all gamers, or anyone interested in the field's history. From the first ever home video game system *Magnavox Odyssey* (1972) to the present day VR technology, exhibits include an array of games, consoles and pop art. There are also temporary exhibitions and events and the chance to play classics of the last forty years.

Parc du Cinquantenaire

7 Parc du Cinquantenaire

MAP H4 ■ Parc du Cinquantenaire, 1000 BRU ■ Musées Royaux d'Art et d'Histoire: 02 741 73 31; open 9:30am–5pm Tue–Fri, 10am–5pm Sat–Sun; closed public hols; adm (free 1–5pm first Wed of month); www.kmkg-mrah.be ■ Musée Royal de l'Armée: 02 737 78 11; open 9am–5pm; closed public hols; adm; www.klm-mra.be ■ Autoworld: 02 736 41 65; open Apr–Sep: 10am–6pm daily, Oct–Mar: 10am–5pm daily (until 6pm on weekends during winter); adm; www.autoworld.be

In 1880 King Léopold II staged a grand international fair to celebrate the 50th anniversary of the founding of his nation. The vast exhibition halls he erected, together with their successors, now contain a cluster of major museums. The most spectacular is the Musées Royaux d'Art et d'Histoire, a collection of treasures from around the world. Close by are the Musée Royal de l'Armée et d'Histoire Militaire (military museum) and Autoworld (collection of vintage cars). The park also contains the Atelier de Moulage, and the Pavillon Horta-Lambeaux, a Neo-Classical work by a young Victor Horta to house an erotic sculpture by Jef Lambeaux (1852–1908).

8 The European Parliament and the Parlamentarium

MAP F5 ■ Rue Wiertz 60, 1047 BRU ■ 02 283 22 22 ■ Multimedia guides: open 9am–1pm Mon–Fri (till 5pm Thu) ■ Parlamentarium: open 1–6pm Mon, 9am–6pm Tue–Fri, 10am–6pm Sat & Sun ■ House of European History: open 1–6pm Mon, 9am–6pm Tue–Fri, 10am–6pm Sat & Sun ■ www.europarl.europa.eu

EU politics may appear to be a complex issue, but a trip to the European Parliament and its House of European History will help you understand European politics like never before. Free audio-guided tours of the Parliament are available, while the Parlamentarium explains

The European Parliament

the past, present and future of the EU in more detail. Visitors are provided with a multimedia handset, which guides them around the interactive displays. Meet the MEPs who shape European laws, listen to the multitude of EU languages in the Tunnel of Voices, and find out why the Parliament decamps from Brussels to Strasbourg every month.

⑨ Meunier Museum

MAP G2 ▪ Rue de l'Abbaye 59, 1050 BRU (Ixelles) ▪ 02 648 44 49 ▪ Open 10am–noon, 12:45–5pm Tue–Fri; closed weekends & public hols ▪ www.fine-arts-museum.be

Constantin Meunier (1831–1905) was one of the great sculptors of the late 19th century, famous for his distinctive bronzes of working people – especially *puddleurs* (forge workers). The museum occupies his former home, and contains some excellent examples of his work.

The Premature Burial, Antoine Wiertz

⑩ Wiertz Museum

MAP F5 ▪ Rue Vautier 62, 1050 BRU (Ixelles) ▪ 02 648 17 18 ▪ Open 10am–noon, 12:45–5pm Tue–Fri; closed public hols & Sat–Sun (except for pre-booked groups) ▪ www.fine-arts-museum.be

This is one of the most extraordinary museums in Brussels. Antoine Wiertz (1806–65) was a controversial artist of the Belgian Romantic movement, who built this grand studio in order to paint giant artworks. These grandiose canvases are interesting, but so too are the smaller works such as his portraits, self-portraits and smaller works, many of which are so macabre and moralistic they inspire both wonderment and mirth.

A WALK THROUGH THE BRUSSELS OF LÉOPOLD II

▶ MORNING

Put on your comfiest walking shoes, because you're going to cover at least 5 km (3 miles) of pavement and take in half a dozen museums. You don't have to do them all, of course, and don't try this on a Monday, when most of the museums are closed. Start at the Schuman métro station in the heart of the European Quarter, close to the Justus Lipsius Building. If you're feeling fit, stride up Rue Archimède to admire the weirdest Art Nouveau building of them all – the **Hôtel Saint-Cyr** in Square Ambiorix *(see p48)*. Otherwise, head into the **Parc du Cinquantenaire** *(see p84)* and take your pick of the museums. To refresh yourself, go to **Place Jourdan**, where there are numerous cafés and restaurants to suit all pockets.

AFTERNOON

Cross the Parc Léopold to visit the **Wiertz Museum**, then walk about 1.5 km (1000 yd) to the trendy **Café Belga** in the 1930s Flagey radio building *(see p87)* for some refreshment. Continue on to the **Meunier Museum** or relax in the arboretum at the neighbouring **Park Tenbosch**. Now you're only 10 minutes away from the **Horta Museum** *(see pp22–3)*. From here you can get a tram home, or wander around the Art Nouveau houses in the vicinity *(see pp48–9)* and finish the day at **Le Clan des Belges** *(see p87)*.

See map on pp82–3 ⟵

The Best of the Rest

① Musée René Magritte

MAP F1 ▪ Rue Esseghem 135, 1090 BRU ▪ 02 428 26 26 ▪ Open 10am–6pm Wed–Sun ▪ Adm ▪ www.magrittemuseum.be

Magritte's modest former abode.

② Musée du Tram

MAP G2 ▪ Ave de Tervuren 364B, 1150 BRU (Woluwe-Saint-Pierre) ▪ 02 515 31 08 ▪ Open Apr–Sep: 1–6pm Sat, Sun & public hols ▪ Adm ▪ www.trammuseum.brussels

A splendid collection of Brussels' historic trams, with tram rides.

③ Béguinage d'Anderlecht

MAP F2 ▪ Rue du Chapelain 8, 1070 BRU ▪ 02 521 13 83 ▪ Open 10am–6pm Tue–Sun ▪ Adm

This *béguinage* (see p92) is a museum showing how the *béguines* lived.

Serres Royales de Laeken

④ Serres Royales de Laeken

MAP G1 ▪ Ave du Parc Royal (Domaine Royal), 1020 BRU ▪ Open three weeks each spring; check website for details ▪ Adm ▪ www.monarchie.be

Fabulous royal greenhouses.

⑤ Maison d'Érasme

MAP F2 ▪ Rue du Formanoir 31, 1070 BRU (Anderlecht) ▪ 02 521 13 83 ▪ Open 10am–6pm Tue–Sun ▪ Adm by reservation only; call ahead ▪ www.erasmushouse.museum

This charming red-brick house where Dutch humanist Erasmus stayed in 1521 is now a museum dedicated to his life.

Muséum des Sciences Naturelles

⑥ Muséum des Sciences Naturelles

MAP F5 ▪ Rue Vautier 29, 1000 BRU ▪ Open 9:30am–5pm Tue–Fri, 10am–6pm Sat, Sun & school hols ▪ Adm ▪ www.naturalsciences.be

See complete dinosaur skeletons.

⑦ Basilique Nationale du Sacré-Coeur

MAP F1 ▪ Parvis de la Basilique 1, 1081 BRU (Ganshoren) ▪ 02 421 16 60 ▪ Rooftop gallery & panorama: open 10am–4:30pm daily (9am–5:30pm in summer) ▪ Church: open 8am–6pm in summer & 8am–5pm in winter

A massive Art Deco building with a remarkable view from its dome.

⑧ Cantillon

MAP A4 ▪ Rue Gheude 56, 1070 BRU (Anderlecht) ▪ 02 521 49 28 ▪ Open 10am–4pm Mon–Sat ▪ Closed Wed, Sun & public hols ▪ Adm (beer tasting included) ▪ www.cantillon.be

A splendid, dusty old brewery.

⑨ Maison Autrique

MAP G2 ▪ Chaussée de Haecht 266, 1030 BRU (Schaerbeek) ▪ Open noon–6pm Wed–Sun ▪ Adm ▪ www.autrique.be

Victor Horta's first project (see p54).

⑩ Africa Museum

MAP H2 ▪ Leuvensesteenweg 13, 3080 Tervuren ▪ 02 769 52 11 ▪ Open 10am–5pm Tue–Fri (till 6pm Sat–Sun) ▪ Adm ▪ www.africamuseum.be

First-class museum (see p64) with exhibitions on African art heritage.

→ *See map on pp82–3*

Restaurants, Cafés and Bars

PRICE CATEGORIES

For a three-course meal for one with half a bottle of wine (or equivalent meal), taxes and extra charges.

€ under €40   €€ €40–60   €€€ over €60

① La Porteuse d'Eau
MAP F1 ▪ Ave Jean Volders 48, 1060 ▪ 02 537 66 46 ▪ Closed Mon ▪ €

Dishes such as steak-*frites* and moules marinières are on offer. Guests can enjoy beer and wine in the Art Nouveau splendour of this famous Saint-Gilles brasserie.

② La Quincaillerie
MAP G2 ▪ Rue du Page 45, 1050 BRU (Ixelles) ▪ 02 533 98 33 ▪ Closed Mon, Sat L ▪ €€

The spectacular Art Nouveau interior of this converted hardware store and the exciting menu more than make up for the occasionally slow service.

③ Le Chapeau Blanc
MAP F2 ▪ Rue Wayez 200, 1070 BRU (Anderlecht) ▪ 02 520 02 02 ▪ Closed Mon ▪ €€

"The White Hat" is a charming brasserie that serves excellent mussels, oysters (in season) and steaks.

④ L'Ultime Atome
MAP D5 ▪ Rue St Boniface 14, 1050 BRU (Ixelles) ▪ 02 513 48 84 ▪ Open daily ▪ €€

Trendy brasserie where locals come to drink artisan beers, cocktails and French red wine.

⑤ Rouge Tomate
MAP C6 ▪ Ave Louise 190, 1050 BRU (Ixelles) ▪ 02 647 70 44 ▪ Closed Sat L & Sun ▪ €€

Dine out on Mediterranean fare, a perfect choice for vegetarians.

⑥ Le Balmoral Milk Bar
MAP G2 ▪ Place Georges Brugmann 21, 1050 BRU (Ixelles) ▪ 02 347 08 82 ▪ Closed Mon & Tue ▪ €

This popular American-style 1960s diner is praised for its burgers and milkshakes.

⑦ La Canne en Ville
MAP G2 ▪ Rue de la Réforme 22, 1050 BRU (Ixelles) ▪ 02 347 29 26 ▪ Closed Sun, Mon, Sat L, & weekends Jul & Aug ▪ €€€

A delightful restaurant in a converted butcher's shop. The cooking is French-based.

⑧ Café Belga (Flagey building)
MAP G2 ▪ Place Eugène Flagey 18, 1050 BRU (Ixelles) ▪ 02 640 35 08 ▪ www.cafebelga.be ▪ €

Trendy café, set in an extraordinary 1930s Art Deco Flagey radio building, that draws a young arty crowd. Also a thriving music venue.

⑨ Moeder Lambic
MAP G2 ▪ Rue de Savoie 68, 1060 BRU (Saint-Gilles) ▪ 02 544 16 99 ▪ €

A welcoming pub devoted primarily to beer, with 450 kinds on offer.

⑩ Le Clan des Belges
MAP D6 ▪ Rue de la Paix 20, 1050 BRU (Ixelles) ▪ 02 511 11 21 ▪ €€

This lively brasserie is very popular with locals for its classic Belgian dishes at reasonable prices.

L'Ultime Atome

🔟 Bruges

In the Middle Ages, Bruges was one of Europe's most prosperous cities. Its wealth derived from trade that brought silks, furs, Asian carpets, wine, fruits, and even exotic pets to its busy network of canals. In about 1500 Bruges fell from grace and slumbered for four centuries. It remained a pocket-sized medieval city, its poverty alleviated by almshouses, pious institutions, and a cottage industry supplying lace. In the late 19th century, antiquarians recognized Bruges as a historic gem, and began a campaign of preservation. In addition to many hotels, restaurants and bars, Bruges has famous art collections, and is a walkable city with surprises on every corner.

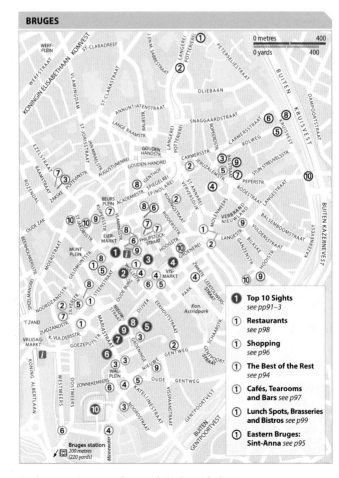

BRUGES

Top 10 Sights
see pp91–3

Restaurants
see p98

Shopping
see p96

The Best of the Rest
see p94

Cafés, Tearooms and Bars see p97

Lunch Spots, Brasseries and Bistros see p99

Eastern Bruges: Sint-Anna see p95

Previous pages Restaurants illuminate the Markt at night, Bruges

Attractive gabled buildings lining the Markt

1 The Markt
MAP K4

The central marketplace of Bruges still retains much of its original outline, flanked by old step-gabled guildhouses, but the Provinciaal Hof (former local government) building on the eastern side is actually 19th century; the left-hand wing now houses the multimedia experience "Historium" (see p94). The Markt is also the site of a large market on Wednesday mornings, and the Christmas market (with an ice rink taking centre stage) in December.

2 Belfort
MAP K4 ▪ Markt 7 ▪ Open 9:30am–6pm daily (Mar–Oct: till 8pm) ▪ Adm

For a breathtaking view over Bruges' medieval streets, climb the 366 steps to the top of the Belfort (belfry). The set of bells at the top includes the 47 carillon bells that are rung by a mechanism installed in 1748. But they can also be played manually from a keyboard on the floor below by the town's *beiaardier* (carillon player) – Bruges' highest paid official, as the joke goes.

3 The Burg

This intimate and fetching square – a glittering confection of historic architecture, sculpture and gilding – was the focal point of old Bruges (see pp28–9).

4 Steenhouwersdijk and Groenerei
MAP L4

Just south of the Burg is one of the prettiest stretches of canal, where calm waters reflect the medieval bridges and skyline. Here, the Steenhouwersdijk (stonemason's embankment) becomes the Groenerei (green canal) and is flanked by a picturesque almshouse called De Pelikaan, dated 1714 and named after the symbol of Christian charity, the pelican.

The canal from Steenhouwersdijk

5 Groeningemuseum

Not only is this one of the great northern European collections, with star roles played by the late medieval masters of Flemish painting, such as Jan van Eyck and Hans Memling; it is also refreshingly compact (see pp30–31).

6 Sint-Janshospitaal

Hans Memling (c. 1430–94) was one of the leading artists of Burgundian Flanders, and the St John's Hospital ranked among his most important patrons. Visitors are advised to use the excellent audio guides available with the entry ticket. The medieval hospital wards display a fascinating miscellany of treasures, paintings and historic medical equipment; there is also a 15th-century pharmacy. The exhibition culminates in the chapel, which contains the hospital's priceless collection of Memling paintings (see pp30–31).

7 Onze-Lieve-Vrouwekerk

MAP K5 ■ Mariastraat ■ Open 9:30am–5pm Mon–Sat (till 1:30pm Fri), 1:30pm–5pm Sun ■ Adm for museum (church free)

The towering spire of the Church of Our Lady (the tallest structure in the city) is another key landmark of Bruges' skyline. It's a strange architectural mishmash: the exterior is a good example of the rather austere style known as Scheldt Gothic, and was built over two centuries from 1220 onward. The interior is essentially Gothic, with Baroque flourishes to its statues and extravagant pulpit (1743). This is a rather surprising

BÉGUINAGES

A feature of the Low Countries, these communities were founded in the 13th century as sanctuaries for the many women (béguines) left single or widowed by the Crusades. Although deeply pious, a béguinage or begijnhof was not a convent: the béguines could leave to marry. Surviving béguinages are still used for social housing, with their modest charms intact (below).

setting for one of the great treasures of northern Europe: Michelangelo's *Madonna and Child* (1504–5) – a Carrara marble statue that came here by virtue of Bruges' close links to Renaissance Italy, and the only sculpture by Michelangelo to leave Italy during his lifetime. The church's museum includes the beautiful gilt-brass tombs of Charles the Bold (1433–77), Duke of Burgundy, and his daughter Mary (1457–82).

8 Arentshuis

MAP K4 ■ Dijver 16 ■ Open 9:30am–5pm Tue–Sun ■ Adm

Born in Bruges, the gifted painter Frank Brangwyn (1867–1956) was the son of William Curtis Brangwyn, one of a group of British artists and architects involved in restoring the city to its Gothic glory. Frank Brangwyn donated an impressive, small, collection of his work to the city. It is now exhibited on the upper floor of the late-18th-century Arentshuis building. The ground floor is used for temporary exhibitions.

Onze-Lieve-Vrouwekerk

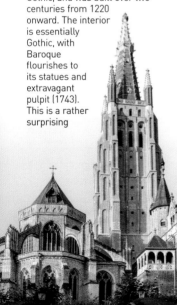

9 Gruuthusemuseum
MAP K4 ■ Dijver 17 ■ Open
9:30am–5pm Tue–Sun ■ Adm

If it is hard to picture quite how life
was led during Bruges' past, this
museum will do much to fill in the
gaps. It presents a rich collection of
everyday artifacts from the homes
of the merchant classes, from kitchen-
ware to musical instruments, furniture
and textiles, and even weapons. The
15th-century building was once
the palace of the Lords of Gruuthuse,
who became wealthy through a tax
on beer flavourings (gruut); as a
mark of their status, the house
has a gallery overlooking the choir
of the Onze-Lieve-Vrouwekerk next
door. The house was restored in the
19th century to exhibit the pieces
that founded this collection.

Gruuthusemuseum

10 Begijnhof
MAP K5 ■ Wijngaardstraat
■ Grounds: open 6:30am–6:30pm
daily; Begijnhuisje: open 10am–
5pm daily ■ Adm to Begijnhuisje
(grounds free)

This beautiful enclave was home to
a community of béguines (see box)
from 1245 until 1928, and expresses
something essential about the soul
of Bruges. Around the peaceful,
tree-shaded park are the 17th- and
18th-century whitewashed homes of
the béguines, and now occupied by
Benedictine nuns. You can visit the
grounds, the béguinage church and
one of the houses (Begijnhuisje).

A DAY IN BRUGES

▶ MORNING

Enjoy a day of wandering,
beginning in the **Burg** (see pp28–
9) and heading south across
Blinde Ezelstraat. Linger beside
the canals on **Steenhouwersdijk**
and **Groenerei** (see p91); walk
through Huidenvettersplein to
the **Dijver** for the prettiest views
of the city. Now make your way
past **Onze-Lieve-Vrouwekerk** to
Mariastraat and **Katelijnestraat**,
where you could stop for a divine
hot chocolate at **De Proeverie**
(see p97). Take Wijngaardstraat
to the **Begijnhof**, loop around the
Minnewater (see p94), and go
back along Katelijnestraat. Note
the almshouses that pop up on
this street (for instance at Nos
87–101 and 79–83). For lunch, try
the **Vismarkt** area – De Gouden
Karpel (see p98) is a good option.

AFTERNOON

Now you are going to pass through
the city's medieval trading centre.
From the **Markt** (see p91) walk
up Vlamingstraat. At **Beursplein**,
there was a cluster of national
"lodges" – headquarters of foreign
traders – such as the **Genoese
Lodge** (No 33). One of Bruges'
more unusual attractions is on
Vlamingstraat: the **Frietmuseum**
(see p94) is dedicated to frites.
Then walk up Langerei to follow
the canal that leads to **Damme**
(see p69), where goods were
transferred from ships to canal
barges. Head back down Sint-
Jakobstraat, and take a detour
to **'t Brugs Beertje** (see p97),
with its famed beers.

See map on p90 ←

The Best of the Rest

1 Sint-Salvatorskathedraal

MAP K4 ▪ Steenstraat ▪ Open 10am–1pm & 2–5pm Mon–Fri (till 3:30pm Sat), 11am–noon & 2–5pm Sun

Art treasures here include late-Baroque bruxellois tapestries and Neo-Gothic stained glass.

2 Sint-Walburgakerk

MAP L3 ▪ Sint-Maartensplein ▪ Open 11am–6pm daily; closed Jan–Mar: Tue–Thu

This handsome Jesuit church, built between 1619 and 1643, is a Baroque symphony in black-and-white marble, with a supreme wooden pulpit.

Beer from Huisbrouwerij De Halve Maan

3 Godshuis De Vos

MAP K5 ▪ Noordstraat 2–8 ▪ Closed to the public

The *godshuizen* (almshouses) of Bruges are easily identified by their humble whitewashed walls, inscribed with names and dates. This delightful example dates from 1643.

Swans on Minnewater lake

4 Minnewater

MAP K6

Romantic, willow-lined lake formed by a sluice gate on the River Reie – a hectic port in medieval times.

5 Diamantmuseum

MAP K5 ▪ Katelijnestraat 43 ▪ 050 34 20 56 ▪ Open 11am–5pm Fri–Sun; closed mid–late Jan ▪ Adm ▪ www.diamond museum.be

The history of diamonds explained. There is a diamond lab that allows visitors to explore the properties of a diamond.

6 Huisbrouwerij De Halve Maan

MAP K5 ▪ Walplein 26 ▪ 050 44 42 22 ▪ Tours 11am–4:15pm daily (till 5pm Sat) ▪ Adm (online booking required) ▪ www.halvemaan.be

Follow the beer-making process at this brewery, in operation since 1856.

7 Frietmuseum

MAP K3 ▪ Vlamingstraat 33 ▪ 05 034 01 50 ▪ Open 10am–5pm daily ▪ Adm ▪ www.frietmuseum.be

This unusual museum is dedicated to the Belgian's adored *frites*.

8 Choco-Story

MAP L3 ▪ Wijnzakstraat 2 ▪ 050 61 22 37 ▪ Open 10am–5pm daily ▪ Adm ▪ www.choco-story-brugge.be

This converted 15th-century *taverne* educates visitors on the production of famous Belgian chocolate.

9 Historium

MAP K4 ▪ Markt 1 ▪ 050 27 03 11 ▪ Open 10am–6pm daily (till 11pm some Sat) ▪ Adm ▪ www.historium.be

A multimedia experience evoking the medieval heyday of Bruges through a tale of young romance.

10 Sint-Jakobskerk

MAP K3 ▪ Sint-Jakobsplein 1 ▪ Open 1–5pm daily

Bruges' richest parish church, it contains notable paintings and tombs.

See map on p90

Eastern Bruges: Sint-Anna

1 Onze-Lieve-Vrouw ter Potterie

MAP L1 ▪ Potterierei 79 ▪ Open 9:30am–12:30pm, 1:30–5pm Tue–Sun ▪ Adm

This charming little museum combines treasures, oddities and an elaborate Baroque chapel.

2 Duinenbrug

MAP L2

Bruges' canals were spanned by charming little drawbridges to allow boats to pass. This one is a reconstruction from 1976.

3 Volkskundemuseum

MAP L3 ▪ Balstraat 43 ▪ Open 9:30am–5pm Tue–Sun ▪ Adm

Occupying eight 17th-century almshouses in the east of the city, Bruges' folk museum presents a fascinating collection of historic artifacts through life-size dioramas.

4 Sint-Annakerk

MAP L3 ▪ Sint-Annaplein ▪ Open 11am–6pm daily; closed Jan–Mar: Tue–Thu

Dominating a tiny square, Sint-Annakerk was elegantly refurbished after destruction by the iconoclasts. The austere building is a tranquil place of worship enlivened by Baroque flourishes.

5 Gezellemuseum

MAP M2 ▪ Rolweg 64 ▪ Open 9:30am–12:30pm & 1:30–5pm Tue–Sun ▪ Adm

Rustic home of one of the best-loved poets in Dutch (and Flemish), the priest Guido Gezelle (1830–99).

6 Schuttersgilde Sint-Sebastiaan

MAP M2 ▪ Carmersstraat 174 ▪ 05 033 16 26 ▪ By appt only ▪ Adm ▪ www.sebastiannsgilde.be

This historic archers' guildhouse still functions as an archery club.

7 Jeruzalemkapel

MAP L3 ▪ Peperstraat 3 ▪ 05 033 88 83 ▪ Open 10am–5pm Mon–Sat (Apr–Sep: till 6pm Sat) ▪ Adm ▪ www.adornes.org

A 15th-century private chapel inspired by pilgrimages to Jerusalem. Next door is the Kantcentrum (Lace Centre).

8 Windmills on the Kruisvest

MAP M2 ▪ Sint-Janshuismolen: open Apr–Sep: 9:30am–12:30pm & 1:30–5pm Fri–Sun ▪ Adm

One of the city's four remaining working flour windmills, Sint-Janshuismolen is open to the public.

9 Kantcentrum

MAP L3 ▪ Balstraat 16 ▪ 05 033 00 72 ▪ Open 10am–5pm Mon–Sat ▪ Adm ▪ www.kant centrum.eu

The Lace Centre explains the history of Bruges' lace, with live demonstrations in the afternoon (Mon–Sat).

10 Kruispoort

MAP M3

One of only four surviving gates of the city walls.

Kruispoort

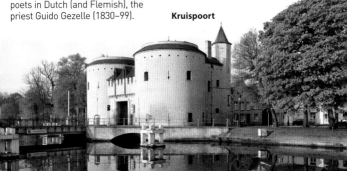

Shopping

Steenstraat and Zuidzandstraat
MAP K4

The main shopping area links the Markt to 't Zand. Clothes, shoes, chocolates – they're all here.

Shoppers on Steenstraat

Zilverpand
MAP K4

This warren of arcades between Zuidzandstraat and Noordzandstraat consists mainly of clothes boutiques.

3 Sukerbuyc
MAP K5 ▪ Katelijnestraat 5

There are chocolate shops at every turn in Bruges, but "Sugarbelly" is family-run and the cocoa treats are handmade on site.

4 The Bottle Shop
MAP K4 ▪ Wollestraat 13

Bruges' De Halve Maan brewery (see p94) produces two beers, Brugse Zot and Straffe Hendrik. You can find them here, along with the full Belgian range.

5 't Apostolientje
MAP L3 ▪ Balstraat 11

There are still some lacemakers in Bruges, though not the 10,000 there were in 1840. A number of lace shops line Breidelstraat between the Markt and the Burg, but this one is the most traditional.

2be
MAP L4 ▪ Wollestraat 53

This shop in a converted 15th-century mayor's house stocks beers, chocolate and biscuits. The bar upstairs offers good canal views.

Huis Van Loocke
MAP L4 ▪ Ezelstraat 17 ▪ Closed Sun & Mon am

Bruges attracts many artists, and several excellent shops cater to their needs. This one has been run by the same family for three generations.

Antiques van Elsen
MAP K4 ▪ Philipstockstraat 13 ▪ Closed Wed pm

A wealth of curios and collectibles from Belgium and across Europe.

Supermarkets
MAP M3 ▪ Langestraat 55

The major supermarkets (such as Louis Delhaize) are in the suburbs, but a few small ones, including Smatch, lie within the city.

10 Markets
MAP J4, K4, L4

General markets are in the Markt (Wednesday mornings) and on 't Zand (Saturday mornings). The Christmas market takes place in the Markt and Simon Stevinplein. Flea markets are held weekend afternoons on Dijver and at the Vismarkt.

Knick-knacks for sale at a market

Cafés, Tearooms and Bars

Funky interior of Duvelorium, run by Belgian brewery Duvel

1 De Garre
MAP K4 ▪ De Garre 1
(off Breidelstraat)
A well-known old *staminee* (pub), hidden down an alleyway. Famous for its strong 11 per cent beer.

2 Café Vlissinghe
MAP L3 ▪ Blekersstraat 2
▪ Closed Mon & Tue
This is said to be the oldest Bruges tavern, founded in 1515. Van Dyck apparently met local painters here. There's a boules court outside.

3 De Proeverie
MAP K5 ▪ Katelijnestraat 6
▪ Open 10am–5pm Tue–Sun
This delightful little coffee shop belongs to the chocolatier opposite: hot chocolate is a speciality.

4 Yesterday's World
MAP K5 ▪ Wijngaardstraat 6
Splendidly quirky pub and cafe, close to the Begijnhof, full of antiques and bric-a-brac for sale.

5 Wijnbar Est
MAP L4 ▪ Braambergstraat 7
▪ 0478 45 05 55 ▪ Closed Mon L, Tue–Thu, Fri L
A tiny, red-brick house that backs onto the canal with live jazz every Sunday from 8pm. Serves Mexican-inspired snacks and an excellent selection of wines.

6 Duvelorium
MAP K4 ▪ Markt 1 ▪ 05 033 53 94 ▪ Open 11am–6pm (till 11pm some Sat)
Part of the Historium (*see p94*), showcasing Belgian beers, with a balcony terrace on the Markt.

7 Joey's Café
MAP K4 ▪ Zilversteeg 4
(off Zuidzandstraat) 16a ▪ 0484 63 05 83 ▪ Closed Sun
A fun café-bar with a friendly staff. Hosts occasional free concerts.

8 't Brugs Beertje
MAP K4 ▪ Kemelstraat 5
▪ 05 033 96 16 ▪ Closed Wed
One of the great beer pubs, serving no fewer than 300 types of beer, including local brews Brugse Zot and Straffe Hendrik.

9 Le Trappiste
MAP K3 ▪ Kuipersstraat 33
▪ Open 5pm–midnight Mon, Tue & Thu (till 1am Fri & Sat)
This atmospheric bar in the brick vaults of a 13th-century cellar serves a broad selection of craft beers on tap.

10 De Republiek
MAP K3 ▪ Sint-Jakobsstraat 36
▪ 050 73 47 64
A large, time-worn bar where the young staff create a vibrant atmosphere. Good for cocktails too.

See map on p90

Restaurants

1 Zet' Joe
MAP L3 ▪ Langestraat 11 ▪ 050
33 82 59 ▪ Closed Sun & Mon ▪ €€€
Run by superstar chef Geert van
Hecke, this restaurant serves
excellent Belgian cuisine.

2 Rock Fort
MAP L3 ▪ Langestraat 15
▪ 050 33 41 13 ▪ Closed Sun, Wed L
& Sat ▪ €€€
Pared-down modern interior in an old
family house. The two young owners
bring flair to the contemporary cuisine.

3 Den Gouden Harynck
MAP L5 ▪ Groeninge 25
▪ 050 33 76 37 ▪ Closed Sun, Mon
& Sat L ▪ €€€
Housed in an attractive 17th-century
house, this is one of Bruges' finest
restaurants. Book ahead.

4 Den Gouden Karpel
MAP L4 ▪ Huidenvettersplein 4
▪ 050 33 34 94 ▪ Closed Sun & Mon
(open Jul–Aug: Sun L) ▪ €€€
A fine fish restaurant beside the
Vismarkt (fish market), with an
excellent fish-shop/*traiteur* next door.

5 Patrick Devos
MAP K4 ▪ Zilverstraat 41
▪ 050 33 55 66 ▪ Closed Sun, Wed D
& Sat L ▪ €€€
An elegant restaurant cherished for
chef Patrick Devos' creative touch.

Outdoor seating at De Stoepa

6 De Stoepa
MAP K5 ▪ Oostmeers 124
▪ 050 33 04 54 ▪ Closed Mon ▪ €
Head to this Mediterranean-style
café to enjoy lunch from a good
menu of tapas, salads and soups.
There's a leafy summer terrace.

7 Assiette Blanche
MAP L4 ▪ Philipstockstraat
23–5 ▪ 050 34 00 94 ▪ Closed Wed &
Thu ▪ €€€
Inventive two-, three- or four-course
menus, with each course designed to
match an accompanying beer.

8 Den Amand
MAP K4 ▪ Sint-Amandsstraat 4
▪ 050 34 01 22 ▪ Closed Sun & Mon
▪ €€
A small restaurant serving inventive
dishes of worldwide inspiration.

9 Den Heerd
MAP L5 ▪ In Hotel Montanus,
Nieuwe Gentweg 76 ▪ 050 35 44 00
▪ Closed Sun, Wed & public hols ▪ €€
Enjoy French and Belgian cuisine
here. You can sit outdoors in the
garden terrace during summer.

10 Bistro de Schaar
MAP M4 ▪ Hooistraat 2 ▪ 050
33 59 79 ▪ Closed Wed & Thu ▪ €€
This snug restaurant is renowned
for its steaks grilled over an open
fire and its homemade desserts.

Belle-époque style at Patrick Devos

Lunch Spots, Brasseries and Bistros

PRICE CATEGORIES
For a three-course meal for one with half a bottle of wine (or equivalent meal), taxes and extra charges.

€ under €40 €€ €40–60 €€€ over €60

1 Bistro de Pompe
MAP K4 ▪ Kleine Sint-Amandsstraat 2 ▪ 050 69 26 86 ▪ Closed Mon ▪ €€

A bistro serving an excellent-value weekday lunch menu. On offer are hearty meals and salads.

Elegant Bistro Christophe

2 Bistro Christophe
MAP L5 ▪ Garenmarkt 34 ▪ 050 34 48 92 ▪ Closed Mon L, Thu & Fri ▪ €€€

Lovely little bistro, which is favoured by locals, serving well-judged Belgian-French cuisine.

3 Locàle by Kok au Vin
MAP K3 ▪ Ezelstraat 21 ▪ 050 33 95 21 ▪ Closed Sun–Tue ▪ €€

This bistro serves sophisticated Belgian snacks and sharing platters in a relaxed and homely atmosphere.

4 Het Paradijs
MAP L4 ▪ Kruitenbergstraat 11 ▪ 050 33 51 16 ▪ Closed D, Sun, Mon ▪ €

Set up to provide inexpensive food for those who need it, this spot features a changing menu with new dishes every day. It also takes on unemployed individuals as chefs to learn a new trade. Takeaway available.

5 De Belegde Boterham
MAP K4 ▪ Kleine Sint-Amands-straat 5 ▪ 050 34 91 31 ▪ Closed Sun ▪ €

A minimalist "lunch boutique" specialising in open sandwiches along with soups, salads and cakes.

6 Belgian Pigeon House
MAP L3 ▪ Sint Jansplein 12 ▪ 050 66 16 90 ▪ Closed Mon L, Tue, Wed & Thu ▪ €€

Set in a brick-vaulted cellar of an old step-gable mansion, this bistro specializes in grilled meats, including pigeon.

7 De Plaats
MAP L4 ▪ Wapenmakersstraat 5 ▪ 050 66 03 66 ▪ Open 11:30am–2pm Mon–Fri ▪ €

This lovely vegan and vegetarian café is housed in the former residence of prolific painter Jacob van Oost.

8 Blackbird
MAP L3 ▪ Jan van Eyckplein 7 ▪ 050 34 74 44 ▪ Closed Mon & Tue ▪ €

Try fresh salads, hearty sandwiches and tea at this elegant and health-conscious spot. Takeaway available.

9 In't Nieuw Museum
MAP M4 ▪ Hooistraat 42 ▪ 050 33 12 80 ▪ Closed Wed & Thu ▪ €€

In this old family-run tavern, the meat is cooked on an open fire (evenings) in a 17th-century fireplace. The atmosphere is traditional and very friendly.

10 Bistro Bruut
MAP L4 ▪ Meestraat 9 ▪ 050 69 55 09 ▪ Closed Sat & Sun ▪ €€€

A canal-side restaurant serving inventive and beautifully presented Flemish dishes made with fresh produce. Booking is essential.

See map on p90

🔟 Antwerp

Exhibit, Museum Aan de Stroom

Set on the Broad River Scheldt, at the gateway to the North Sea, Antwerp is one of the leading trading cities of northern Europe; and in the early 17th century it was one of the great cultural centres too. The city has had its share of suffering – battered by the religious wars of the 16th century, cut off from the North Sea by treaty with the Netherlands from 1648 to 1795, and bombed in World War II. These historical ups and downs have endowed the city with a keen edge, like its famous diamonds. This dynamic energy is seen today in its hip bars, restaurants and nightclubs.

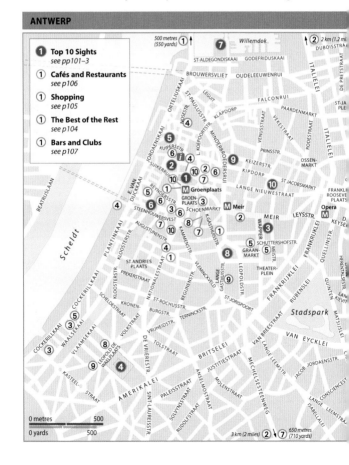

ANTWERP

- **1** Top 10 Sights
  see pp101–3
- **1** Cafés and Restaurants
  see p106
- **1** Shopping
  see p105
- **1** The Best of the Rest
  see p104
- **1** Bars and Clubs
  see p107

1 Antwerp Cathedral

This huge Gothic cathedral, a city landmark, contains several splendid works by Rubens *(see pp32–3)*.

2 Grote Markt

MAP T1 ▪ Stadhuis: guided tours only, book three weeks ahead (ask at tourist office, Grote Markt 1; for guided tours in English call 03 205 56 05) ▪ Adm

The main square of Antwerp is one of the great gilded arenas of Belgium. The city authorities commissioned sculptor Jef Lambeaux (1852–1908) to create an eye-catching fountain, placed

Grote Markt with its central fountain

off-centre, with its water spilling out onto the cobbles. It depicts Brabo, a legendary Roman soldier who freed the port of Antwerp by defeating the giant Antigoon and throwing his severed hand *(hand-werpen)* into the river. The Italian-influenced Stadhuis (city hall) dominates the square. Built in the 1560s, its grand horizontals are offset by the upward curve of the roof-corners.

3 Rubenshuis

MAP U2 ▪ Wapper 9–11 ▪ 03 201 15 55 ▪ www.rubenshuis.be

This magnificent 17th-century patrician house was once the home and studio of one of the great stars of European art. It will be closed for extensive renovation from 2023 until 2027.

View from the gardens, Rubenshuis

4 Koninklijk Museum voor Schone Kunsten (KMSKA)

MAP S3 ▪ Leopold de Waelplaats ▪ 03 224 95 50 ▪ www.kmska.be

Antwerp's fine arts museum *(see pp34–5)* is second only to Brussels' with its full range of paintings, from early Flemish "Primitives" to the Symbolists.

Museum Vleeshuis

⑤ Museum Vleeshuis
MAP T1 ■ Vleeshouwerssstraat 38 ■ 03 292 61 01 ■ Open 10am–5pm Thu–Sun ■ Adm ■ www.museum vleeshuis.be

With its turrets and towers and Gothic detail, the "Meat House" is one of the most beautiful buildings of Antwerp. Built in 1501–4 as the guildhouse of the butchers and a meat market, it is now used as a museum of music. The Museum Vleeshuis charts the history of the city through its many forms of musical expression, using historical instruments, including harpsichords made by the famous Ruckers family, manuscripts and a bell foundry.

⑥ Museum Plantin-Moretus
MAP T2 ■ Vrijdagmarkt 22 ■ 03 221 14 50 ■ Open 10am–5pm Tue–Sun; closed public hols ■ Adm (free last Wed of month) ■ www. museumplantinmoretus.be

Christophe Plantin (c.1520–89) was a French bookbinder who, in 1546, came to Antwerp to set up his own printing workshop. It became one of the most influential publishing houses in Europe during the late Renaissance, producing Bibles, maps, scientific books and much more. The museum is a UNESCO World Heritage Site, and consists essentially of the printing workshop and home of Plantin and his heirs. It contains a large collection of rare and precious books, and displays of their illustrations.

⑦ Museum Aan de Stroom (MAS)
MAP T1 ■ Hanzestedenplaats 1 ■ 03 338 44 00 ■ Open 10am–5pm Tue–Sun; closed public hols ■ Adm (free last Wed of month) ■ www.mas.be

It is impossible to miss this towering museum built of red sandstone and perspex. Through its collection of ethnographic and folkloric treasures, MAS explores Antwerp's rich history, art and culture, and the city's interaction with the rest of the world.

⑧ Museum Mayer van den Bergh
MAP T2 ■ Lange Gasthuisstraat 19 ■ 03 338 81 88 ■ Open 10am–5pm Tue–Sun ■ Adm (free last Wed of month) ■ www.museummayer vandenbergh.be

Fritz Mayer van den Bergh (1858–91) was an avid collector of art and curios. When he died, his mother

Museum Mayer van den Bergh

created a museum to display his collections – some 5,000 items in all. They include tapestries, furniture, stained glass, paintings and coins.

9 Snijders-Rockoxhuis

MAP U1 ▪ Keizerstraat 10–12
▪ 03 201 92 50 ▪ Open 10am–5pm Tue–Sun; closed some public hols ▪ Adm (free last Tue of month) ▪ www.snijdersrockoxhuis.be

Come here for a glimpse of the grace and elegance of 17th-century patrician style. The museum occupies the houses of the city mayor Nicholas Rockox (1560–1640), a philanthropist and a friend and patron of Rubens, as well as the artist Frans Snijders (1579–1657), who lived next door. There is a fine collection of furniture, paintings and artifacts, including works by Snijders himself.

Stained-glass detail, Sint-Jacobskerk

10 Sint-Jacobskerk

MAP U2 ▪ Lange Nieuwstraat 73–75 ▪ 048 60 55 43 ▪ Open 2–5pm daily; closed some public hols ▪ Adm

Of all the churches in Antwerp, the church of St James is noted for having the richest interior – and for being the burial place of Rubens. It was built in late Gothic style in the 15th and 16th centuries by architects who also worked on the cathedral. The church contains work by leading sculptors of the 17th century, such as Lucas Faydherbe and Hendrik Verbruggen, as well as paintings by Rubens, Jordaens and Van Dyck.

A DAY IN ANTWERP

▶ MORNING

This day of gentle ambling takes in many of the key sights of Antwerp, as well as some of the best shopping streets. Start off at the **Museum Vleeshuis** and head for the old city centre – the **Grote Markt** (see p101) – and the cathedral (see pp32–3). Thread your way to Wijngaardstraat, and the fetching ensemble of the **Sint-Carolus Borromeuskerk** (see p104), before heading on to the **Snijders-Rockoxhuis** in Keizerstraat. After this, walk south along Katelijnevest to the **Meir**. The tower block to your right, with KBC on its crest, is the **Boerentoren**, the highest building in Europe when constructed in 1932. Head down the Meir past the **Rubenshuis** (see p101), and have lunch at the Art Nouveau **Grand Café Horta** (see p106).

AFTERNOON

Now you've done the culture, you can wander the neighbourhood's shopping streets (see p105). **Schuttershofstraat** is a good place to start. It leads to Huidevettersstraat, the Nieuwe Gaanderij Arcade, Korte Gasthuisstraat and Lombardenvest. If you are in the mood for more museums, the excellent **Museum Mayer van den Bergh** and the **Maagdenhuismuseum** (see p104) are just to the south. Or head for Nationalestraat and Dries van Noten's outlet, the beautiful **Het Modepaleis**, (see p105), and then down to **Mooy** (see p106) or **Billie's Bier Kafétaria** (see p106) for refreshment.

See map on pp100–101 ←

The Best of the Rest

Red Star Line Museum exhibits

1 Red Star Line Museum
MAP T1 ▪ Montevideostraat 3
▪ 03 298 27 70 ▪ Open 10am–5pm
Tue–Sun; closed public hols
▪ Adm ▪ www.redstarline.be

Between 1873 and 1934, Red Star
ocean liners departed from Antwerp's
docks for the United States, taking
families to a new life. This museum
explores their journey.

2 Middelheim Museum
Middelheimlaan 61 ▪ 03 288
33 60 ▪ Open Apr & Sep: 10am–7pm
Tue–Sun (May–Aug: till 8pm; Oct–Mar:
till 5pm); closed public hols

High-quality open-air sculpture
park, with hundreds of modern
and contemporary pieces.

3 FotoMuseum Provincie Antwerpen (FoMU)
MAP S3 ▪ Waalsekaai 47 ▪ 03 242
93 00 ▪ Open 10am–6pm Tue–
Sun ▪ Adm ▪ www.fomu.be

Antwerp's excellent
museum of photography
and historical artifacts has
ever-changing exhibitions.

4 Sint-Pauluskerk
MAP T1 ▪ Veemarkt 13
▪ 03 232 32 67 ▪ Open
Apr–Oct: 2–5pm daily
(Nov–Mar: Sat & Sun)

Gothic and Baroque fight
it out alongside artworks by Rubens
and Van Dyck.

5 M HKA
MAP S3 ▪ Leuvenstraat 32
▪ 03 260 99 99 ▪ Open 11am–6pm
Tue–Sun; closed public hols
▪ Adm ▪ www.muhka.be

A former warehouse is home to
the cutting-edge Museum van
Hedendaagse Kunst, which is
all about contemporary art.

6 Sint-Carolus Borromeuskerk
MAP T1 ▪ Hendrik Conscienceplein
12 ▪ 03 231 37 51 ▪ Open 10am–
12:30pm, 2–5pm Mon–Sat; for
religious services Sun

This church is renowned for its
Baroque façade and its tragic loss of
39 Rubens' paintings in a fire in 1718.

7 De Koninck Brewery
Mechelsesteenweg 291
▪ 03 866 96 90 ▪ Open 9am–7pm
daily (last entry 6pm) ▪ Adm
▪ www.dekoninck.be

Visitor centre and tours at Antwerp's
most famous brewery.

8 Cogels-Osylei
In the late 19th century,
this street became a showcase for
opulent architecture – some of the
examples are quite extraordinary.

9 Maagdenhuismuseum
MAP U3 ▪ Lange Gasthuisstraat
33 ▪ 03 435 99 10 ▪ Open 10am–
1pm & 2–5pm Tue–Sun; closed
public hols ▪ Adm

This quirky museum, with
some lovely old masters, is
set in an old orphanage.

Porridge bowl, Maagdenhuismuseum

10 ModeMuseum MoMu
MAP T2 ▪ Nationalestraat
28 ▪ 03 470 27 70 ▪ Open
10am–6pm Tue–Sun
▪ Adm ▪ www.momu.be

A museum of *haute
couture* presenting
fashion in its social, political and
cultural context.

Shopping

1 Nieuwe Gaanderij Arcade
MAP T2 ■ Between Huidevettersstraat and Korte Gasthuisstraat

A good place to seek out fashion at a slightly lower price than the usual designer boutiques.

Meir, busy with shoppers

2 Meir
MAP U2

The main shopping street is a broad pedestrianized avenue, fronted largely by high-street chain stores.

3 Grand Bazar Shopping Center
MAP T2 ■ Beddenstraat 2

An elegant modern arcade shares space with the Hilton hotel in the shell of a former department store.

4 Nationalestraat
MAP T2

The heart of Antwerp's *haute couture* fashion district offers boutiques by many world-class designers but remains accessible to all.

5 Schuttershofstraat
MAP U2

Another street of recherché boutiques and shoe shops, including a branch of the ultimate Belgian accessories manufacturer Delvaux – you can smell the leather.

6 Het Modepaleis
MAP T2 ■ Nationalestraat 16

This elegant *belle époque* "flat iron" building is the main outlet for one of Antwerp's most fêted fashion designers, Dries van Noten.

7 Louis
MAP T2 ■ Lombardenstraat 2

This boutique was originally established to sell clothes by the popular "Antwerp Six" and other local fashion designers. It now promotes the work of final year fashion students as well.

8 Ann Demeulemeester
MAP S3 ■ Leopold de Waelplaats/Verlatstraat

Only a short distance from the M HKA contemporary art gallery, Demeulemeester's shop displays the uncompromising edge that has placed her at the forefront of fashion.

9 Grand Diamonds
MAP V2 ■ Vestingstraat 69

Diamonds at lower prices than elsewhere in Europe. At the same time as purchasing that special ring, you can learn about diamonds.

Diamond shop in Pelikaanstraat

10 Pelikaanstraat
MAP V2

Wall-to-wall diamond and jewellery shops in the Jewish quarter. Fascinating, partly because there's nothing romantic about it – the gems are commodities like any other.

See map on pp100–101 ←

Cafés and Restaurants

1 Huis de Colvenier
MAP T2 ▪ Sint-Antoniusstraat 8
▪ 0477 23 26 50 ▪ €€€

This is one of the most respected restaurants in Antwerp, so you should book in advance.

2 De Peerdestal
MAP T1 ▪ Wijngaardstraat 8
▪ 03 231 95 03 ▪ €€€

Set in a medieval horse stable, this restaurant is well-known for its fish and lobster menus.

3 Billie's Bier Kafétaria
MAP T2 ▪ Kammenstraat 12
▪ 03 226 31 83 ▪ Open 4pm–midnight Mon–Thu, 2pm–midnight Sun (till 1am Sat); closed Tue

A traditional "brown pub" serving hearty regional fare, washed down by a choice of 180 craft beers.

4 RAS
MAP S2 ▪ Ernest van Dijckkaai 37 ▪ 03 234 12 75 ▪ €€€

A landmark building looming over the River Scheldt. Home to an elegant, first-class brasserie.

5 Grand Café Horta
MAP U2 ▪ Hopland 2
▪ 03 203 56 60 ▪ €€

A dynamic space created using metal salvaged from Victor Horta's celebrated Art Nouveau Volkshuis (Brussels), demolished in 1965.

The rosy, pink interior of Mooy

6 Mooy
MAP T2 ▪ Lombardenvest 19
▪ 03 422 65 29 ▪ Closed D & Sun

This quirky café serves vegan-friendly dishes, organic wines and irresistible homemade cakes.

7 Günther Watté
MAP T2 ▪ Steenhouwersvest 30 ▪ 03 293 58 94 ▪ Closed Mon ▪ €

With its renowned pralines made in-house, this café is a favourite with connoisseurs of coffee and chocolate.

8 Pannenkoekenhuis De Famille Suykerbuyck
MAP T2 ▪ Reyndersstraat 18 ▪ 03 866 31 61 ▪ Closed Mon & Tue ▪ €

Sweet and savoury pancakes in a grand 17th-century convent, with a delightful courtyard. There's also a hot chocolate menu.

9 Dôme Sur Mer
Arendstraat 1 ▪ 03 281 74 33 ▪ Closed Sat L ▪ €€

Floor-to-ceiling windows and a marble bar make an impressive setting for this popular fish restaurant.

10 Brasserie Appelmans
MAP T2 ▪ Papenstraatje 1
▪ 03 226 20 22 ▪ Closed Mon & Tue ▪ €€

Inventive Belgian and international dishes served inside a beautifully renovated 19th-century building; also home to "Absinthbar".

Grand Café Horta interior

Bars and Clubs

1 Appleman's Absinthbar
A part of Brasserie Appelmans (see p106), this bar is among the most famous absinthe and cocktail bars in Belgium. DJs play on some weekends.

2 IKON
Kotterstraat 1 ▪ **03 295 54 65**

Hip nightclub, a taxi ride away in the northern Het Eilandje district.

3 Café Local
MAP S3 ▪ **Waalsekaai 25**
▪ **03 446 01 35**

A glamorous party complex with themed Latin-American-style areas, in a 19th-century warehouse setting.

Interior of Het Elfde Gebod

4 Het Elfde Gebod
MAP T1 ▪ **Torfbrug 10**
▪ **03 288 57 33**

Quirky, yet cosy, bar where the walls are decked with gaudy religious icons. Head here to enjoy delectable Belgian cuisine and a variety of beers.

5 Copa Cava
MAP T2 ▪ **Vlasmarkt 32**
▪ **0494 60 89 36** ▪ **Closed Mon & Tue**

Cosy Spanish-style bodega serving reasonably priced Cava, either by the "copa" or by the bottle.

6 Den Engel
MAP T1 ▪ **Grote Markt 3**
▪ **03 233 12 52**

A classic Belgian pub overlooking the Grote Markt. Try a *bolleke* (chalice-like glass) of De Koninck, Antwerp's own brew.

Den Engel in Grote Markt

7 De Muze
MAP T2 ▪ **Melkmarkt 15**
▪ **03 226 01 26**

A friendly pub where you can listen to live jazz most evenings until 2 or 3am. Exposed beams and brickwork create an intimate atmosphere.

8 Ampere
MAP V3 ▪ **Simonsstraat 12**
▪ **03 232 09 23** ▪ **Closed Sun–Thu**

This popular techno nightclub, under the railway tracks near the station, draws a young crowd.

9 Café Hopper
MAP S3 ▪ **Leopold de Waelstraat 2** ▪ **03 248 49 33**

This jazz bar is very popular with Antwerp's creative set. Ask for a *"half en half"*: half cava; half white wine.

10 Cocktails at Nine
MAP T2 ▪ **Lijnwaadmarkt 9**
▪ **03 344 79 54** ▪ **Closed Tue & Wed**

Stylish spot with wood-beamed ceilings and smooth stone floors. Enjoy cocktails on the two patios in summer or by the open fire in winter.

See map on pp100–101

🔟 Ghent

Ghent has much in common with Bruges. It is a city with a rich legacy of medieval buildings and art treasures inherited from its days as a semi-autonomous and prosperous trading centre. The tranquil waters of its canals mirror the step-gables of its old guildhouses and the tall spires of its three famous towers. Unlike Bruges, however, historically prosperous Ghent took on a new lease of life as Belgium's first industrial city in the early 19th century. It is also home to a large university. These factors have endowed the city with a scale, bustle and youthful verve that have shaped its character. Ghent has a grandeur, symbolized by its cathedral, theatres and opera house, but it also has an intimacy, and the web of its medieval streets – including Europe's largest pedestrianized zone – makes this a perfect city for wandering.

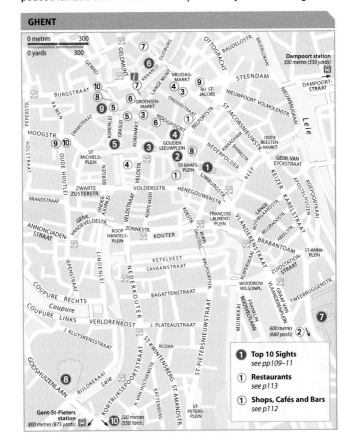

GHENT

🔲	**Top 10 Sights** see pp109–11
①	**Restaurants** see p113
①	**Shops, Cafés and Bars** see p112

The stunning altar, Sint-Baafskathedraal

3 Sint-Niklaaskerk

MAP Q2
■ Cataloniëstraat
■ 09 234 28 69 ■ Open
10am–4pm daily

St Nicholas, Bishop of Myra, was patron saint of merchants, and this was the merchants' church. Built in the 13th to 15th centuries, in Tournai bluestone, it is Belgium's best example of the austere style called Scheldt Gothic (named after the Scheldt river).

1 Sint-Baafskathedraal

MAP Q2 ■ Sint-Baafsplein
■ 09 397 15 00 ■ Open 8:30am–
5:30pm Mon–Sat, 1–5:30pm Sun;
Ghent Altarpiece: open 10am–5pm
Mon–Sat, 1–5pm Sun (only
open to non-worshippers
after 1pm Sun) ■ Adm (Mystic
Lamb only)

St Bavo was a local 7th-century saint. The cathedral named after him dates back to the 10th century, but most of it is Gothic, built over three centuries after 1290. Highlights include the grandiose Baroque-Rococo pulpit of oak and marble (1741–5) and the church's greatest treasure the multi-panelled, 15th-century altarpiece, *The Adoration of the Mystic Lamb* by Hubrecht and Jan van Eyck *(see pp36–7).*

2 Belfort

MAP Q2 ■ Sint-Baafsplein
■ 09 233 39 54 ■ Open 10am–6pm
daily (last adm at 5:30pm) ■ Adm

Ghent's belfry is a prominent landmark, rising 91 m (299 ft) to the gilded dragon on the tip of its spire. It was built between 1313 and 1381 and served for centuries as look-out tower, clock and alarm. It houses a 54-bell carillon, which is used for regular concerts. There is a lift to transport visitors to the top.

4 Stadhuis

MAP Q2 ■ Botermarkt 1
■ Book tour in advance from the
tourist office ■ Adm

Standing on the main square is the impressive town hall. It has a series of regal council chambers, still in use today – some dating back to the 15th century, others refurbished during restoration after 1870.

Detail on the wall, Stadhuis

5 Graslei and Korenlei

MAP P2

The Graslei and Korenlei are departure points for canal trips. The two quays are lined with the step-gabled guildhouses of merchants and tradesmen that date back to the 12th century. Sint-Michielsbrug, the bridge at the southern end, offers the best views of the city.

The quay, Graslei

Exhibit in the Huis van Alijn

6 Huis van Alijn

MAP Q1 ■ Kraanlei 65 ■ 09 235 38 00 ■ Open 9am–5pm Mon, Tue, Thu & Fri, 10am–6pm Sat & Sun; Jul & Aug: 10am–6pm daily ■ Adm

Just north of the centre of Ghent is a quaint quarter called the Patershol, a warren of little medieval streets and alleys (see p54). This is the backdrop for one of the best folk museums in Belgium. An intriguing collection of everyday objects from the recent and distant past – toys, record covers, games, shoes and crockery – are laid out within almshouses, which are set around a grassy courtyard. These almshouses were founded in 1363 as a children's hospital – not as an act of pure philanthropy but as penance for the murder of two members of the Alijn family.

7 Klein Begijnhof

MAP R4 ■ Lange Violettestraat 235 ■ Open 6:30am–10pm daily

There are three béguinages (see p92) in Ghent, but this is by far the prettiest. With step-gabled, whitewashed brick houses set around a little park and Baroque church, it has earned the status of a UNESCO World Heritage Site. It was founded as a community of single women in about 1235, and has been continuously occupied, although the residents are no longer béguines. Most of the present houses date from the 17th century.

8 STAM

MAP P4 ■ Godshuizenlaan 2 ■ 09 267 14 00 ■ Open 9am–5pm Mon–Fri, 10am–6pm Sat, Sun & school hols; closed Wed ■ Adm ■ www.stamgent.be

The Abdij de Bijloke, an old rambling Cistercian abbey and hospital, provides a superb setting for STAM, Ghent's City Museum. Covering the history of the city from prehistoric times to the present day, STAM incorporates the vast range of items of the former Bijloke Museum, including medieval tombs, freemasons' regalia and models of warships. The abbey dates from medieval times, but most of the buildings are from the 17th century.

GHENT AND CHARLES V

Charles V (1500–58), Holy Roman Emperor, King of Spain, master of much of Europe and the Americas, was born in Ghent, and his baptism in Sint-Baafskathedraal was celebrated with a huge feast. But the city's love affair with its famous son went sour when it found itself endlessly squeezed for taxes. A revolt in 1540, and the execution by hanging of its ringleaders, gave rise to the people of Ghent being called the *stroppendragers* ("noose bearers") – a proud symbol of their defiant and independent spirit.

Antique map of Ghent, STAM

9 Design Museum Gent

MAP P1 ∎ Jan Breydelstraat 5
∎ 09 267 99 99 ∎ Closed for renovation
∎ Adm ∎ www.designmuseumgent.be

Scheduled to reopen in 2024
following renovations, this museum
is a must for anyone with the
slightest interest in furniture,
furnishings and interior decoration.
Housed in a grand 18th-century
mansion, plus an uncompromisingly
modern extension, it provides a tour
through changing European styles
from the 17th century to the present.
The Art Nouveau collection is particularly rewarding, with work by Horta,
Paul Hankar and René Lalique.

Exhibits, Design Museum Gent

10 Museum voor Schone Kunsten (MSK) and SMAK

MAP Q6 ∎ Citadelpark ∎ MSK: 09 323
67 00; www.mskgent.be; SMAK: 09
240 76 01; www.smak.be ∎ Open
9:30am–5:30pm Tue–Fri (till 10pm
first Thu of every month), 10am–6pm
Sat, Sun, public hols & school hols;
closed Mon ∎ Adm

Ghent's two leading museums of
art lie south of the city centre. The
MSK (Fine Arts Museum) covers
painting and sculpture from the
Middle Ages up to the early 20th
century and has an eclectic collec-
tion of works by artists such as
Hieronymus Bosch, Rogier van der
Weyden and Hugo van der Goes.
Opposite the MSK is the Stedelijk
Museum voor Acktuele Kunst (SMAK),
Ghent's superb modern art gallery
featuring a permanent collection –
with pieces by Magritte and Marcel
Broodthaers – and regularly
changing temporary exhibitions.

A DAY IN GHENT

▶ MORNING

SMAK and the **Museum voor
Schone Kunsten** make a good
double act – a stimulating mixture
of fine art and pure provocation,
from world-class artists. Get
these under your belt early in
the day (note that they're closed
on Mon). Tram 1 runs from the
central Korenmarkt (Cornmarket)
to Charles de Kerchovelaan, from
where you can walk through or
beside the Citadelpark to the
museums. These will absorb
the greater part of the morning;
you can break for refreshments
at SMAK's café. For lunch, head
back into the city centre. The
Korenmarkt is equidistant from
two enticing and contrasting
lunch options: **Maison Elza**
(see p113), and the medieval
Groot Vleeshuis *(see p112)*.

AFTERNOON

Visit **Sint-Baafskathedraal** to see
the **Mystic Lamb** *(see pp36–7)*.
Then climb up the **Belfort** *(see
p109)* to get a view over the city.
Now it's back to the Korenmarkt,
with a stop at the **Sint-Niklaaskerk**
(see p109), then over to the **Graslei**
and **Korenlei** *(see p109)* to take
in the views. This could be the
ideal time to take a canal trip.
From the Korenlei, walk along
Jan Breydelstraat and take the
first right into Rekeligestraat
to reach the **Gravensteen**. Then
cross the Zuivelbrug and take
Meerseniersstraat to the
Vrijdagmarkt (Friday Market)
square for beer at **Dulle Griet**
(see p112) and chips at **nearby**
Frituur Bij Sint-Jacobs *(see p113)*.

See map on p108

Shops, Cafés and Bars

1 Mageleinstraat and Koestraat
MAP Q2

Ghent city centre has an extensive pedestrianized zone, which makes shopping here all the more agreeable. Most chain stores are in Lange Munt and Veldstraat, but there's more charm around the quieter Mageleinstraat and Koestraat.

2 Markets
www.visitgent.be/en/markets

There is a market every day in Ghent (six on Sunday): a Sunday walking tour can take you to them all.

3 Tierenteyn-Verlent
MAP Q1 ▪ Groentenmarkt 3 ▪ Closed Sun

On the go since 1790, this delicatessen is famous for its homemade mustard that is pumped up from the cellars into a wooden barrel.

Herbs and spices, Tierenteyn-Verlent

4 Dulle Griet
MAP Q1 ▪ Vrijdagmarkt 50

One of the celebrated "beer academies" of Belgium, with 500 beers on offer. Note the basket in which you must deposit a shoe as security when drinking a "Max" beer, served in its own unique glass.

5 Het Spijker
MAP P2 ▪ Pensmarkt 3–5

Cosy candle-lit bar in the cellar of a 13th-century leprosy shelter, with a large, popular terrace.

Butcher's hall, Groot Vleeshuis

6 Groot Vleeshuis
MAP Q1 ▪ Groentenmarkt 7 ▪ 09 223 23 24 ▪ Closed Mon ▪ €

This centre for Eastern Flemish food – part restaurant, part delicatessen – is sensationally located in a medieval butchers' hall.

7 't Dreupelkot
MAP Q1 ▪ Groentenmarkt 12

A waterfront bar serving only *jenever*, a form of gin, variously flavoured with fruit, vanilla and even chocolate.

8 Brooderie Jaffa
MAP P1 ▪ Jan Breydelstraat 8 ▪ Closed Mon & Tue ▪ €

The tempting smell of freshly baked bread wafts around this rustic-style spot, which serves sandwiches, snacks and light vegetarian fare.

9 Hotsy Totsy
MAP P2 ▪ Hoogstraat 1 ▪ 09 224 20 12 ▪ €

Atmospheric 1930s decor and evenings of jazz, poetry and cabaret make this legendary Ghent bar worth seeking out.

10 Café Labath
MAP P2 ▪ Oude Houtlei 1 ▪ €

A popular locals café serving excellent coffee and hot chocolate, as well as delicous breakfasts, soups and sandwiches. Friendly service.

Restaurants

PRICE CATEGORIES
For a three-course meal for one with half a bottle of wine (or equivalent meal), taxes and extra charges

€ under €40   **€€** €40–60   **€€€** over €60

1 De Rave
MAP Q2 ▪ Schepenhuisstraat 2 ▪ 09 225 96 60 ▪ Closed Tue & Wed ▪ €€

Housed in a stylish 17th-century building near the Stadhuis, this restaurant offers Franco-Belgian cuisine with a modern twist.

2 Bar Bask
MAP R4 ▪ Edward Pynaertkaai 115 ▪ 09 311 69 74 ▪ Closed L, Sat & Sun

Basque-inspired restaurant, serving tapas and *pintxos*. Every dish is an artwork. Booking essential.

3 Keizershof
MAP Q1 ▪ Vrijdagmarkt 47 ▪ 09 223 44 46 ▪ Closed Sun, Mon & L ▪ €€

A good list of mainly classic Belgian dishes is served in this lively brasserie, on several floors.

4 Brasserie Pakhuis
MAP P2 ▪ Schuurkenstraat 4 ▪ 09 223 55 55 ▪ Closed Sun ▪ €€

Run by the Portuguese restaurant designer Antoine Pinto, Pakhuis is big and very popular – so reserve!

5 Korenlei Twee
MAP P2 ▪ Korenlei 2 ▪ 09 224 00 73 ▪ Closed Sun & Mon ▪ €€€

This 18th-century dockside town house, serves meals using ingredients from the local fish and meat markets. Good value and excellent wine too.

6 Mosquito Coast
MAP Q2 ▪ Hoogpoort 28 ▪ 09 224 37 20 ▪ €

Laidback travellers' café adorned with souvenirs from around the world. It offers world cuisine with good vegetarian options, shelves of guidebooks and two sunny terraces.

7 Karel de Stoute
MAP Q1 ▪ Vrouwebroersstraat 2 ▪ 09 224 17 35 ▪ Closed Sat L, Sun, Mon ▪ €€€

Named after Charles the Bold, Duke of Burgundy, this is a highly respected gourmet restaurant in the Patershol district. Set menus only, permitting the chefs to excel.

8 Brasserie De Foyer
MAP Q2 ▪ Sint-Baafsplein 17 ▪ 09 234 13 54 ▪ Closed Mon, Tue ▪ €€

This excellent brasserie is dramatically located within the grand 19th-century Koninklijke Nederlandse Schouwburg (theatre), with a balcony overlooking Sint-Baafskathedraal.

9 Frituur Bij Sint-Jacobs
MAP Q1 ▪ Vrijdagmarkt

A popular chip stand serving the perfect chips (frites), twice fried, and all the trimmings late into the night.

10 Maison Elza
MAP P1 ▪ Jan Breydelstraat 36 ▪ 09 225 21 28 ▪ Closed Tue, Wed ▪ €€€

Set in a lovely spot overlooking the canal, this restaurant serves top-notch Belgian cuisine.

Rustic interior of Brasserie Pakhuis

See map on p108

Streetsmart

Galeries Royales Saint-Hubert, Brussels

Getting Around

Arriving by Air

Most international flights arrive at Brussels airport, located at Zaventem 14 km (9 miles) northeast of Brussels. **Ryanair** flies to Charleroi (Brussels South), which is 60 km (37 miles) south of the city, as well as to Zaventem.

From **Brussels Airport**, there are taxi services into town, but the easiest and most economic way to reach central Brussels is by train, with around three trains per hour. Tickets are on sale in the airport complex or can be purchased online; the journey to Gare Centrale takes 20 minutes. There are onward links from Brussels to Bruges, Antwerp and Ghent.

A bus service called Airport Line, run by STIB/MIVB, connects the airport to Brussels' European Quarter. From **Charleroi Airport**, there are shuttle buses to Brussels, and a regular bus service direct to Bruges and Ghent; you can also take the bus to the railway station at Charleroi-Sud, then the train to Brussels, Bruges, Antwerp or Ghent.

Antwerp Airport also operates international flights connecting to London Southend, London City Airport and a limited number of other European destinations.

Arriving by Sea

Travellers from Britain can cross the English Channel by ferry, or via the Channel Tunnel. Ferries from Dover land at Calais or Dunkirk (in France), both of which lie fairly close to the Belgian border. There is also a longer crossing to Belgium itself: **P&O Ferries** operates an overnight crossing between Hull and Zeebrugge. These services are all geared to passengers travelling with cars. Individual foot passengers will need to arrange a way to get to and from the ferry ports.

Arriving by Train

The central hub of Belgium's rail network is Brussels, which has three main stations: the Gare du Midi (or Zuidstation), the Gare Centrale (Centraal Station) and the Gare du Nord (Noordstation). Both the **Eurostar** and high-speed **Thalys** services operate out of the Gare du Midi, which is served by metro trains, buses and trams.

Eurostar trains run hourly between London's St Pancras International station and Brussels via the Channel Tunnel; the journey takes just under 2 hours. Passengers should arrive at the terminal a minimum of 30–40 minutes before departure to go through the check-in and customs procedures before boarding. (It is possible that you may be refused access to the train if you arrive after this time, although you can often be transferred to the next service at no extra charge.) Tickets usually include the cost for travelling from Brussels to other Belgian stations (e.g. Bruges, Antwerp or Ghent), valid for 24 hours after your arrival; a return from the destination is likewise valid for 24 hours before your departure back home from Brussels.

The Thalys network connects Brussels with Paris (accessible in 1 hour and 25 minutes), Amsterdam (around 2 hours) and Cologne (under 3 hours).

From Brussels, there are good local train connections to Bruges, Ghent and Antwerp.

Arriving by Coach

Eurolines, a group of companies forming Europe's largest coach network, operates services from Victoria Coach Station in London to Brussels' Gare du Nord, via the Channel Tunnel. Prices are extremely competitive compared to other forms of travel to Brussels, though this is offset by a journey time of around 7 hours. From Gare du Nord, the centre can be reached either by mainline SNCB trains, Pre-Metro trams or city buses. Eurolines also operates direct services from London to Ghent and Antwerp.

Flixbus runs a service to Brussels from London's Victoria Coach Station. Coaches arrive at Brussels North station or the Gare du Midi, with excellent metro, bus and tram links to the rest of the city. It also runs regular coach services to Bruges, Antwerp and Ghent.

Arriving by Car

To bring a car into Belgium, you must carry a valid EU driving licence, or international driving licence, plus insurance and car-registration documents. You must also carry a warning triangle, first-aid kit and fluorescent safety jacket with you in the car.

Le Shuttle, operated by **Eurotunnel**, takes vehicles from the Channel Tunnel entrance near Folkestone direct to Calais, a journey of about 35 minutes. (It is advisable to book tickets in advance and try to arrive early.) From there, Brussels is just a 2-hour drive via the A16 motorway, which becomes the E40 when you cross the Franco-Belgian border. Follow signs first to Brugge (Bruges), and then on to Brussels.

You will be driving on the right, so if you are travelling from Britain make sure to adjust the angle of your headlamps, or use patches, so that they don't dazzle oncoming drivers. All the motorways in Belgium are toll-free and most are well maintained. Almost all are very well lit at night.

Distances Between Cities

Belgium is small – hardly larger than Wales or New Hampshire – and the four cities are all in the north of the country. Brussels is the farthest south; Antwerp lies 55 km (34 miles) due north of Brussels; Ghent lies to the west and about 50 km (31 miles) from Brussels and Antwerp; Bruges lies a further 40 km (25 miles) northwest of Ghent.

Local Trains

Run by **Belgian National Railways** – known as Société Nationale Chemins de Fer Belges (SNCB) in French and Nationale Maatschappij der Belgische Spoorwegen (NMBS) in Dutch – Belgium's train network provides a fast and economical means of travelling between all four cities.

Fares for standard second-class tickets are calculated by distance, so return tickets generally offer no savings and are usually valid only until midnight. Children aged under six travel free, with a maximum of four children allowed per adult, and those aged between six and 11 receive a 50 per cent discount. Special tariffs are available for under-26s and senior citizens.

A variety of rail passes are available for more extensive travel. These include the Rail Pass, which allows ten trips within Belgium over one year. SNCB is part of the Interrail network of train companies across Europe. Travellers can use the Interrail Pass to travel around Belgium and beyond.

Car Rental

All the main car-hire agencies operate in Belgium, although renting a vehicle can be expensive. To hire a car, you must be 21 or over, with a year's driving experience, and be in possession of a credit card. Usually you get better value if you book a hire car in your home country, linking it with your flight. Note, however, that all the cities are compact; you don't really need a car to get around unless you want to go touring outside the city limits.

Rules of the Road

Belgians drive on the right-hand side of the road. Speed limits are 50 kph (30 mph) in built-up areas, 120 kph (75 mph) on motorways and dual carriageways and 90 kph (55 mph) on all other roads. These limits are reduced to as low as 20 kph in some residential areas and near schools. There are motorway links between all the cities; these are fast, reasonably well maintained and toll-free. It is worth getting breakdown coverage before you leave. Break-down services are offered by the two main Belgian motoring organizations: **Touring** and **VAB**.

There is plenty of parking in and around all the cities; the best plan is to head for one of the main public car parks, which are well signposted. Traffic in city centres, especially Bruges and Ghent, can be bad so visitors are encouraged to use outlying car parks and walk or take the park-and-ride bus. If you are staying overnight, check in advance if your hotel has private parking; this may be relatively expensive, but has the merit of convenience.

Public Transport

Within the cities, the main transport systems are bus and tram; Brussels also has the Metro (an underground railway or subway), and Brussels and Antwerp both have an underground tram system called the Pre-Metro. Public transport in Brussels is operated by **STIB** (in Dutch **MIVB**); in the other cities the operator is **De Lijn**.

Tickets

Tickets for public transport cover buses, trams and the metro. Single tickets, day passes and preloadable multi-journey **MOBIB** Basic cards can be bought at ticket booths or stations. Single tickets for buses and trams are also available from the driver. Children under six with a paying adult can travel for free (up to four children per adult). At the start of a journey, validate the ticket or card (in the orange machine or on the red contact pad) on board a bus or tram, or on entering a Metro station; it is then valid for a single journey of up to an hour, including any changes you need to make.

Buses

All bus stops should be treated as request stops, and drivers need to be signalled to when a person wants to board. Similarly, the on-board buttons are used to indicate that passengers wish to get off at the next stop.

In addition to public bus services, Bruges and Brussels both offer sightseeing tours by bus, with recorded commentaries. This is a hop-off, hop-on service, and tickets are valid for 24 hours.

Trams

As well as bus services, Brussels, Ghent and Antwerp all have trams. Running on dedicated lines that are usually (although not always) free of road traffic, they have the advantage of following a reliable published schedule, and move swiftly through the city streets even at rush hour. Maps of the network and ticket offices make planning a journey fairly easy. As with buses, all stops are request stops; equally, the bell-button must be pressed for disembarking.

Metro

The Brussels Metro provides quick transport around the city centre and to the suburbs in all directions. Stations are marked by signs with a blue "M" on a white background. Scheduled services run from 6am to midnight (with shorter hours at weekends or on public holidays). The Pre-Metro service in Brussels and Antwerp, where the tram network travels through extensive underground tunnels in the city centre, functions much like the regular Metro system.

Taxi

Taxis are available at taxi ranks – usually found in strategic locations such as outside railway stations or close to the central square – or can be booked by phone. All taxis have a rooftop sign that is illuminated when the vehicle is vacant. In Brussels, cabs can occasionally be hailed on the street – but not usually in the other three cities. They cost quite a lot more than public transport. Taxi drivers do not necessarily have a detailed and precise knowledge of their city, so it helps to come armed with full information about the destination. The price of a journey always includes service, though it is quite normal to round up the total fare.

Canal Boats

The city best known for its canals is Bruges – this is why it is sometimes referred to (misleadingly) as the Venice of the North. From March to November (and at weekends in winter), tour boats leave from various points in the city centre, and make tours of varying length around the extensive canal network – a delightful way to see the city from a quite different perspective. One useful tip is to take an umbrella if it has been raining, as the bridges drip. Ghent also has canals, although rather less extensive than those of Bruges. They again show the city in an agreeably tranquil light.

Cycling

Belgians are keen cyclists and traffic is usually respectful. However, the cycling experience can vary depending on the city you are in. Thousands of students pedal around Ghent, for instance, while the old streets of central Bruges have relatively light and slow-moving traffic. Brussels by contrast is a rather more challenging proposition, with congested, busy, cobbled streets filled with parked cars, trams and

frustrated drivers. That said, there are plenty of people who do cycle in Brussels, and who take advantage of recommended cycle routes.

You can hire bikes in all the cities; tourist offices (see p121) will be able to provide details of hire companies. There are also several bike-sharing schemes available. **Blue-bike** is a nationwide service managed by the national railway company SNCB, and Antwerp has **Velo Antwerpen**. Bikes can be hired by the day or week, paying online or at one of the cycle stations. Blue-bikes must be returned to the original location (otherwise you will be charged an extra fee), but Velo Antwerpen bikes can be returned to any of the stations. In Brussels, bicycles can be taken on the Metro except at rush-hour.

Beyond the cities, the flat landscape in much of Flanders is ideally suited to touring by bicycle, with a well-signposted network of cycle paths. Tourist offices and cycle-hire shops can provide information on routes.

Walking

Walking is by far the best way to get around; in all the cities, the main sights are central, and all within easy walking distance. Town planners have generally shown great consideration for pedestrians, with broad pavements and plenty of street crossings; Brussels, Antwerp and Ghent all have extensive pedestrianized zones around the main areas.

Traffic is meant to stop for walkers at zebra-crossings, but this may not always happen. Some crossings also have traffic signals, and drivers will follow them, not a pedestrian's wish to cross: it is best to wait for the green man to light up. Sturdy walking shoes are recommended to cope with the many cobbled streets that can be found in all four cities.

Away from the cities, Belgium offers a range of hiking excursions, from one-day adventures to multi-day long-distance routes. The country is notably crossed by the long-distance, transnational GR 5 trail, which links the Netherlands to the Mediterranean via Liège and Luxembourg.

DIRECTORY

RULES OF THE ROAD

Touring
w touring.be

VAB
w vab.be

PUBLIC TRANSPORT

De Lijn
w delijn.be

STIB/MIVB
w stib-mivb.be

TICKETS

MOBIB
w stib-mivb.be

CYCLING

Blue-bike
w blue-bike.be

Velo Antwerpen
w velo-antwerpen.be

Practical Information

Passports and Visas

For entry requirements, including visas, consult your nearest Belgian embassy or check the **Belgian Immigration Office** website. You need a passport to enter Belgium, valid at least three months beyond the end of your stay. Citizens of the EU, the UK, USA, Australia and New Zealand do not need a visa if staying for less than 90 days. Citizens of other countries should consult their nearest Belgian embassy for information. Brussels is the "Capital of Europe", so most major countries have embassies in the city – and most of them are located in and around the European Quarter to the east of the centre.

Government Advice

Now more than ever, it is important to consult both your and the Belgian government's advice before travelling. The **UK Foreign and Commonwealth Office**, the **US Department of State**, the **Australian Department of Foreign Affairs and Trade** and the **Belgian Federal Public Service Foreign Affairs** office offer information on security, health and local regulations.

Customs Information

You can find information on the laws relating to goods and currency taken in or out of Belgium on the **Belgian Federal Public Service Finance** website. Most goods can be transported between EU countries, including wines, beer, spirits and tobacco, provided they are for your own personal use, and in quantities that reflect this. For non-EU citizens flying into and out of Belgium, national limits apply.

Insurance

We recommend that you take out a comprehensive insurance policy covering theft, loss of belongings, medical care, cancellations and delays, and read the small print carefully. UK citizens are eligible for free emergency medical care in Belgium provided they have a valid European Health Insurance Card (**EHIC**) or UK Global Health Insurance Card (**GHIC**). Under 75 per cent of specified costs can be reclaimed; you usually have to pay for medical treatment in the first instance and reclaim costs later, so be sure to keep all your receipts.

Australia has a reciprocal health care agreement with Belgium and citizens can access essential medical treatment as long as they are registered to Medicare.

Health

Belgians enjoy a high standard of healthcare; their hospitals – usually located in modern buildings situated in spacious grounds in the suburbs on the periphery of the cities – rank among the best in Europe. This healthcare is extended to foreign visitors, but you will have to pay for it if you are not properly covered by insurance.

Should you suffer an accident or illness, or need emergency dental treatment, ask locally about how best to access these services; for example, hotels have lists of duty doctors and dentists. Pharmacists are readily available and can give advice and over-the-counter medication – for Belgians, they are often the first port of call for treatment of minor ailments and injuries. Each city has a rota of late-night pharmacies.

In general, health hazards are few and the tap water is safe to drink. For information about COVID-19 vaccination requirements, consult government advice.

ID

Note that you are obliged by law to carry an identity document (for example, a passport or driver's licence) at all times. The police are entitled to ask you to produce this for inspection, but they cannot take it away from you.

Smoking, Alcohol and Drugs

Smoking and vaping are officially forbidden in confined public places and on public transport. They are also prohibited in restaurants and cafés (unless they have a dedicated smoking area, or food represents less than one-third of their business and they have special permission). Smoking may be tolerated in smaller bars.

Beer and wine may be purchased by anyone over the age of 16, while stronger spirits (15 per cent or more) can only be bought by those aged 18 or over.

All drugs are prohibited by law in Belgium.

Personal Security

Belgium is generally safe, but petty crime does take place. Brussels Midi station in particular has a reputation for pickpockets and theft. Use your common sense, keep valuables in a safe place, and be alert to your surroundings. If you are the victim of a crime, report it to the police – within 24 hours in the case of theft – if you wish to claim on insurance. Many police officers

speak English, and you are likely to get a very professional response.

As a rule, Belgians are very accepting of all people, regardless of their race, gender or sexuality. Homosexuality has been legal since 1795 and in 2003, Belgium became the second country in the world to legalize same-sex marriage. If you do feel unsafe, the **Safe Space Alliance** pinpoints your nearest place of refuge.

Ambulance, **police**, and **fire services** are reliable and can be called for free from any landline, mobile or phonebooth.

Travellers with Specific Requirements

Belgium is full of historic buildings, steps, kerbs, narrow doors and cobbled streets, but little has been done to the physical environment to accommodate people with reduced

mobility. Although improvements are being made, accessible facilities in hotels, restaurants and public places are far from uniform, so it is wise to phone ahead. Local tourist offices can advise disabled travellers; **Visit Flanders** in particular has a wealth of information on its website, including advice for travellers with visual and hearing impairments. The **Brussels For All** website is another useful source of advice for travellers with specific requirements, as is **Handy.Brussels**.

Time Zone

Belgium is on Central European Time (CET), one hour ahead of Greenwich Mean Time (GMT). It observes Daylight Saving Time, moving the clocks forward in late March and back in late October.

DIRECTORY

PASSPORTS AND VISAS

Belgian Immigration Office
w dofi.ibz.be

TRAVEL SAFETY ADVICE

Australian Department of Foreign Affairs and Trade
w dfat.gov.au/travel
w smartraveller.gov.au

Belgian Federal Public Service Foreign Affairs
w diplomatie.belgium.be

UK Foreign and Commonwealth Office
w gov.uk/foreign-travel-advice

US Department of State
w travel.state.gov

CUSTOMS INFORMATION

Belgian Federal Public Service Finance
w finance.belgium.be

INSURANCE

EHIC
w ec.europa.eu

GHIC
w gov.uk/global-health-insurance-card

PERSONAL SECURITY

General Emergency
(112

Ambulance and Fire Services
(112

Police
(101

Safe Space Alliance
w safespacealliance.com

TRAVELLERS WITH SPECIFIC REQUIREMENTS

Brussels For All
w be.brussels/culture-tourism-leisure/brussels-for-all

Handy.Brussels
w handy.brussels/en/

Visit Flanders
w visitflanders.com/en/accessibility

Money

Belgium's currency is the euro (€). Bank and credit cards can be used to draw cash from ATMs, which are widespread. Most major credit and debit cards are accepted in shops, restaurants and hotels, though reluctance may be shown towards American Express.

Tipping is not common in Belgium. A service charge is included in restaurant prices, but customers can leave a small extra tip (by rounding up the bill or adding 10 per cent) if service has been particularly good. The service is also included in taxi fares, although it is normal to round up the fare by up to 10 per cent.

Electrical Appliances

Belgium runs on 230 volts AC, using the round two-pin plugs that are common across mainland Europe. The current is fine for the majority of British equipment just to require an adaptor, but American visitors will need a transformer too.

Mobile Phones and Wi-Fi

Mobile-phone coverage is good, especially in the cities. Visitors travelling to Belgium with EU tariffs can use their devices without being affected by data roaming charges. Visitors from other countries should check their contracts before departure in order to avoid incurring unexpected charges.

Just about all hotels now offer free Wi-Fi for those using their mobile phones or laptops; some also have computer terminals that guests can use in their lobbies. Free or paid-for Wi-Fi access is also available in many bars and cafés.

Postal Services

Post offices are generally open Mon–Fri 9am–5pm. You can buy stamps there and ascertain postage rates for heavier and international items. Main post offices have *poste restante* and banking facilities.

Stamps are also available from some tobacconists, newsagents and shops selling postcards. Post boxes are red, often adorned with a post horn and crown, and normally have a label announcing the usual collection times.

Weather

Belgian weather is typical for northern Europe: a mix of sun and rain, distributed across the four seasons. Average seasonal temperatures range from 1°C (34°F) in winter to 19°C (66°F) in summer. All seasons have their merits: summer is most likely to have the best weather, but spring and autumn can be sunny as well as warm. Winter can be bitterly cold, but the towers and steeples of the city skylines can light up spectacularly in the low-angled sun, and all the cities host Christmas markets to bring seasonal cheer to December.

Regarding clothing and what to pack, assume the worst in weather and you'll be fine. Think in terms of multiple layers, so you can adapt to all weather conditions, and always carry a waterproof one. Be sure to pack stout and comfortable shoes: walking is the best way to see the cities. Bring a compact umbrella that can be easily stored in a backpack or bag.

Opening Hours

As a general rule, shops are open from 10am to 6pm; small shops such as bakeries and newsagents often open earlier. Some shops close for lunch but stay open later in the evening. On Sundays, pâtisseries, chocolate shops, delicatessens, tourist shops, and small and central supermarkets remain open. Some shops stay open late on one night of the week.

Banks are generally open Mon–Fri 9am–noon and 2–4pm, but some larger branches do not close for lunch. Some banks also open on Saturday mornings. The exchange bureaus have longer opening hours, and may be open through the weekend.

Belgian public holidays are: New Year's Day; Easter Monday; Labour Day (1 May); Ascension Day (6th Thu after Easter); Whit Monday (7th Mon after Easter); Flanders Day (11 July); National (Independence) Day (21 July); Assumption (15 Aug); All Saints' Day (1 Nov); Armistice Day

(11 Nov); and Christmas Day. Although banks and post offices will remain closed, some museums and shops may stay open.

COVID-19 Increased rates of infection may result in temporary opening hours and/or closures. Always check ahead before visiting museums, attractions and hospitality venues.

Visitor Information

Each city has its own tourist office – **Visit Brussels**, **Visit Bruges**, **Visit Antwerp** and **Visit Ghent** – providing detailed local information and assisting with hotel reservations. All of these tourist offices have useful websites providing details of key attractions, festivals, events, restaurants and hotels, as well as maps, other useful information and links. The regional tourist office, **Visit Flanders**, is also a useful source of information on both the cities and the wider Flanders area.

Local Customs

In certain dishes, beef is served raw. This applies to Steak Américain, minced beef – not quite what it might sound like to the uninitiated.

Belgian beers are often somewhat stronger than their equivalents in Britain and the USA, and range from about 5 per cent to 12 per cent alcohol by volume (sometimes even

more). Since beers are generally served in fairly small quantities, the effect can be deceptive – until you stand up.

It is worth noting that it is illegal in public places to wear clothing that either largely or completely hides a person's face. Those wearing such clothing (e.g. the burka and nikab) risk a fine and/or detention for up to seven days.

Language

The people of Flanders (which includes Bruges, Antwerp and Ghent) speak Dutch (Nederlands); this may be informally referred to as Flemish (Vlaams), but the official language is categorically Dutch. In Brussels the people speak mostly French or Dutch.

Generally, English is fairly widely understood; in Flanders many people prefer to speak in English rather than French, even though it is one of the Belgian national languages. German is also an official language, but this is spoken primarily in the eastern regions.

Taxes and Refunds

The standard VAT rate in Belgium is 21 per cent, which applies to most goods and services. Visitors from outside the EU staying fewer than three months may claim the VAT back on purchases over €125. A Tax-Free form must be completed in the store, a copy of which is given to the customs authorities on departure, along with proof of purchase.

Accommodation

Accommodation is of a high standard, from the top five-star and boutique hotels to budget options and bed-and-breakfast stays. Prices tend to reflect the ebb and flow of business and holiday trade. Summer is busy in Bruges, but less so in Brussels, Antwerp or the university city of Ghent. Note that the prices quoted may not always include city or tourism tax, which is usually €2 extra per person per night.

Places to Stay

PRICE CATEGORIES

For a standard double room per night (with breakfast if included), including taxes and extra charges.

€ under 150   €€ €150–275   €€€ over €275

Brussels Hotels: Top of the Range

Brussels Marriott Hotel Grand Place

MAP B2 ■ Rue Auguste Orts 3–7, 1000 BRU ■ 02 516 90 90 ■ www. marriott.com ■ €€

A Marriott with unique character, located near the Bourse and the Grand Place. Ideal for business, shopping and leisure.

The Dominican

MAP C2 ■ Rue Léopold 9, 1000 BRU ■ 02 203 08 08 ■ www.thedominican.be ■ €€

Set on a quiet street right behind Theatre Royal de la Monnaie and within walking distance of the Grand Palace, this luxurious hotel is one of the best in the city. Award winning architects have created a pleasant private courtyard over which the rooms look, and a sumptuous Grand Lounge.

The Hotel

MAP C5 ■ Boulevard de Waterloo 38, 1000 BRU ■ 02 504 11 11 ■ www. thehotel-brussels.be ■ €€

This high-rise may not look much from the outside, but the inside is brimming with surprises, including contemporary decor and stunning views from the higher rooms, as well as the 23rd-floor sauna and gym. Excellent service.

Steigenberger Wiltcher's

MAP C6 ■ Avenue Louise 71 ■ 02 542 42 42 ■ www. steigenberger.com ■ €€€

Set in the suburb of Ixelles, on one of Brussels' most exclusive shopping boulevards, this grandiose hotel features elegant, spacious rooms. It also has a sophisticated spa with an infinity pool, and deluxe service – all meriting its five-star status. Look out for good value offers in low season.

Manos Premier

MAP C6 ■ Chaussée de Charleroi 100–106, 1060 BRU ■ 02 537 96 82 ■ www.manospremier. com ■ €€

A privately owned five-star boutique hotel offering 50 rooms styled with period furniture, an on-site spa and a restaurant. The reception has an old Parisian-style feel with marble and gilt-edged mirrors. Guests can also enjoy the peaceful private garden. Very calm yet close to the bustling Avenue Louise.

Radisson Blu Royal

MAP C2 ■ Rue Fossé-aux-Loups 47, 1000 BRU ■ 02 219 28 28 ■ www. radissonblu.com ■ €€

The foyer, showcasing the work of renowned Belgian architect Michel Jaspers, is breathtaking – a towering atrium, with tropical plants and fountains filling its base, and glass-fronted lifts rising into the firmament. The hotel has a smart cocktail bar, which is open daily.

Sofitel Brussels Le Louise

MAP C6 ■ Avenue de la Toison d'Or 40, 1050 BRU ■ 02 514 22 00 ■ www.accorhotels.com ■ €€

Don't be deterred by the fact that this is a chain hotel, Sofitel brought in revered designer Antoine Pinto to redefine this five-star hotel with a glamorous, eclectic vibe. Rooms are plush, and the restaurant has a lovely sunny terrace.

Warwick Brussels

MAP C3 ■ Rue Duquesnoy 5, 1000 BRU ■ 02 505 55 55 ■ www. warwickhotels.com ■ €€

Equidistant from the Grand Place and the Musées Royaux des Beaux-Arts, this elegant and sumptuous hotel is part of the Warwick group. It has a restaurant, bar and fitness suite.

Amigo

MAP B3 ■ Rue de l'Amigo 1–3, 1000 BRU ■ 02 547 47 47 ■ www.roccoforte hotels.com ■ €€€

Steps away from the Grand Place, this smart hotel occupies the site of a 16th-century prison. Rooms are decked out in rich Flemish fabrics, and Tintin prints adorn the bathroom walls.

Stanhope

MAP E5 ▪ Rue du Commerce 9, 1000 BRU ▪ 02 506 91 11 ▪ www.thonhotels.com ▪ €€€
Located just around the corner from the Royal Palace, this hotel is decorated in an English country house-style. It offers old-fashioned services and elegant rooms, and has a beautiful interior garden. It also houses a gourmet restaurant and a fitness centre. Free Wi-Fi available.

Brussels: Hotels of Character

Espérance

MAP C1 ▪ Rue du Finistère 1–3, 1000 BRU ▪ 02 219 10 28 ▪ www.hotel-esperance.be ▪ €
This 1930s Art Deco gem is hidden away near Place des Martyrs (see p76). Most rooms are modern, but Room 7 still retains its old splendour. The tavern/breakfast room has hardly changed and is a must for evening drinks.

Meininger

MAP A2 ▪ Quai Hainaut 33, 1080 BRU ▪ 02 588 14 74 ▪ www.meininger-hotels.com ▪ €
Housed in a former brewery, this trendy, carbon-neutral, three-star hotel has over 170 fun rooms, including family rooms. There are also bikes available for hire.

Hotel Barsey by Warwick

Avenue Louise 381–3, 1050 BRU ▪ 02 641 51 30 ▪ www.warwickhotels.com/barsey ▪ €€
Located at the southern end of stylish Avenue Louise, this hotel was decorated by French designer Jacques Garcia in an opulent Edwardian style. The rooms exude a sense of luxurious, silky comfort. The private terrace is a bonus in summer.

Hotel Bloom

MAP E1 ▪ Rue Royale 250, 1210 BRU ▪ 02 220 66 11 ▪ www.nh-hotels.com ▪ €€
A bright, fresh, modern hotel; all-white rooms each with a fresco painted by a young European artist. Set behind the botanical gardens with easy access to the Gare du Nord and the city centre.

Ibis Styles Brussels Louise

MAP C6 ▪ Avenue Louise 212, 1050 BRU ▪ 02 644 29 29 ▪ www.ibis.com ▪ €€
Once independently run, the former White Hotel is now part of the Ibis chain, but it retains its contemporary all-white theme and continues to showcase artwork of young Belgian designers.

Le Dixseptième

MAP C3 ▪ Rue de la Madeleine 25, 1000 BRU ▪ 02 517 17 17 ▪ www.ledixseptieme.be ▪ €€
There is no other place quite like this in Brussels: an utterly charming and fascinating small hotel in the late-17th-century residence of the Spanish ambassador. It has a number of suites ingeniously set beneath the roof beams, and furnished with a mixture of antique charm and modern flair.

Le Plaza

MAP C1 ▪ Boulevard Adolphe Max 118–26, 1000 BRU ▪ 02 278 01 00 ▪ www.leplaza-brussels.be ▪ €€
Feel like Louis XVI's guest in the palatial foyer and public rooms of this grand hotel, with its stucco, gilt, and lavish ceiling paintings. The guest rooms maintain the same high standard of spacious comfort.

Odette en Ville

MAP D8 ▪ Rue de Châtelain 25, 1050 BRU ▪ 02 640 26 26 ▪ www.odetteenville.be ▪ €€
An intimate eight-room boutique hotel located in a 1920s building. Rooms are decorated with calming greys and whites, and have fixtures such as underfloor heating. There is an on-site restaurant with open fire.

The Manos Premier

MAP C6 ▪ Chausée de Charleroi 100-106, 1060 BRU (Saint-Gilles) ▪ 02 537 96 82 ▪ www.manospremier.com ▪ €€
This hotel is beautifully furnished with chandeliers and antique furniture. It has a Turkish-inspired hammam, gourmet restaurant, bar and spacious garden.

Vintage Hotel

MAP C6 ▪ Rue Dejoncker 45, 1060 BRU ▪ 02 533 99 80 ▪ www.vintagehotel.be ▪ €€
Close to Avenue Louise, this 1960s-styled boutique hotel has rooms with bubble lamps and psychedelic wallpaper, and an option to "glamp" in an Airstream campervan. At night, the breakfast room turns into a wine bar.

Brussels Hotels: Business and Budget

2GO4 Grand Place

MAP C3 ■ Boulevard Emile Jacqmain 99, 1000 BRU ■ 02 219 30 19 ■ www.2go4.be ■ €

Just around the corner from the Grand Place, this hostel has options to suit all budgets, the range of rooms on offer includes multi-share rooms, singles and doubles, with or without private bathrooms. There are excellent kitchen facilities and free internet access.

Aloft Brussels Schuman

MAP G4 ■ Place Jean Rey, 1040 BRU ■ 02 800 08 88 ■ www.aloftbrussels.com ■ €€

Funky, affordable boutique-design hotel in the heart of the EU district. Instead of a restaurant, there is a 24-hour "food station" serving snacks, sandwiches, salads and treats, as well as drinks. A choice of breakfast options is also available. Other facilities include free Wi-Fi, a fitness centre and a bar with live music.

Aqua Hotel

MAP D5 ■ Rue de Stassart 43, 1050 BRU ■ 02 213 01 01 ■ www.aqua-hotel-brussels.com ■ €€

Located in a quiet street close to the Metro, this crisp, clean, good-value hotel is popular with businesspeople looking for something a bit different – a huge, blue Arne Quinze sculpture twists through the entire building.

Marivaux

MAP C1 ■ Boulevard Adolphe Max 98, 1000 BRU ■ 02 227 03 00 ■ www. hotelmarivaux.be ■ €€

A simple but satisfactory business hotel with contemporary-styled guest rooms and state-of-the-art meeting rooms. Relax in the cocktail bar or enjoy a fusion-cuisine meal in the elegant brasserie.

NH Brussels EU Berlaymont

MAP G3 ■ Boulevard Charlemagne 11–19, 1000 BRU ■ 02 231 09 09 ■ www.nh-hotels.com ■ €€

Close to the heart of European government, this eco-friendly hotel is favoured by diplomats, politicians and journalists. They make full use of its state-of-the-art communication systems, fitness centre, Turkish baths and sauna.

Pillows City Hotel Brussels Centre

MAP D3 ■ Rue des Paroissiens 15–23 ■ 02 274 08 10 ■ €€

Tucked away in the shadow of the Cathédrale des Saints Michel et Gudule, and close to the central station, this hotel offers small but stylish rooms. It also has a suite of salons for business meetings, a cosy bar and a café.

The Progress Hotel

MAP G1 ■ Rue du Progrès 9, 1210 BRU ■ 02 205 17 00 ■ www.progresshotel. be ■ €€

Friendly, small hotel close to the Botanical Gardens with functional black-and-white rooms. After a day of business

meetings, guests can relax on massage chairs in the covered winter garden with its 100-year-old olive trees. Airport pickups and customized tours can be arranged through the concierge.

Radisson Red Brussels

MAP E5 ■ Rue d'Idalie 35, 1050 BRU ■ 02 626 81 11 ■ www.radissonred.com ■ €€

A deluxe hotel adjacent to the European Parliament, with spacious designer bedrooms, premier meeting rooms, sauna, fitness centre and Willards bar/restaurant.

Sofitel Brussels Europe

MAP G5 ■ Place Jourdan 1, 1040 BRU ■ 02 235 51 00 ■ www.accor hotels.com ■ €€

Elegant five-star hotel just a stone's throw from the European Parliament. The spacious rooms are beautifully designed in contemporary style, and feature luxury bathrooms that come with designer toiletries. Extras include 11 meeting rooms, a hammam, a fitness centre, a rooftop terrace and an on-site chocolate shop for last-minute gifts.

Thon Hotel EU

MAP F4 ■ Rue de la Loi 75, 1040 BRU ■ 02 204 39 11 ■ www.thonhotels. com ■ €€

This multi-coloured hotel offers functional, modern rooms, free Wi-Fi, a fitness centre with gym and sauna, a restaurant and fully-equipped conference rooms.

Bruges Hotels: Luxury

De Castillion

MAP K4 ▪ Heilige Geeststraat 1 ▪ 05 034 30 01 ▪ www.castillion.be ▪ €€

Occupying a 17th-century bishop's residence in the west of the city, this comfortable hotel has imaginatively decorated bedrooms and bathrooms. The high standard of the rooms is matched by its remarkable Art Deco lounge and bar.

Crowne Plaza Hotel

MAP L4 ▪ Burg 10 ▪ 05 044 68 44 ▪ www.ihg.com ▪ €€

Set at the very heart of Bruges, the Crowne Plaza overlooks the Burg. A modern establishment, it also incorporates some historic remains: the excavated foundations of the medieval church of St Donatian. The hotel has an indoor swimming pool, the PlazaCafé and its own car park.

Die Swaene

MAP L4 ▪ Steenhouwersdijk 1 ▪ 05 034 27 98 ▪ www.dieswaene.be ▪ €€

An opulent, romantic hotel with rooms in the 18th-century building and in the modern "pergola" looking out over the pretty canal. Amenities include a glamorous lounge in an old guildhall, an indoor swimming pool and a gastronomic restaurant.

Heritage

MAP K3 ▪ Niklaas Desparsstraat 11 ▪ 05 044 44 44 ▪ www.hotel-heritage.com ▪ €€

Located in a 19th-century mansion, in the old merchant quarter to the north of the Markt, this hotel houses the restaurant Le Mystique, plus a spa and a fitness room in its 14th-century cellar, and a sun deck with city views on the roof.

Hotel Aragon

MAP K3 ▪ Naaldenstraat 22 ▪ 05 033 35 33 ▪ www.aragon.be ▪ €€

A well-presented and well-managed hotel close to the centre. It's part of the Swan Hotel Collection, which includes the Dukes' Palace. The hotel also has eight apartments nearby, which can accommodate up to seven people.

Hotel Dukes' Palace

MAP K4 ▪ Prinsenhof 8 ▪ 05 044 78 88 ▪ www.hoteldukespalace.com ▪ €€

This former ducal palace has definitely earned its five stars thanks to the spa pool, art gallery and chapel. The Manuscript restaurant serves a great breakfast. The bar is not cheap, but locals seem to think it's worth it.

Hotel de Orangerie

MAP K4 ▪ Kartuizerinnenstraat 10 ▪ 05 034 16 49 ▪ www.hotelorangerie.be ▪ €€

Housed in a 15th-century convent, this hotel has a gorgeous panelled breakfast room and lounge with a terrace overlooking the canal. It exudes character and charm.

NH Brugge

MAP J5 ▪ Boeveriestraat 2 ▪ 05 044 97 11 ▪ www.nh-hotels.com ▪ €€

Once a 17th-century monastery, this building retains some lovely features, such as stained-glass windows, large fireplaces and wooden beams. The rooms are in a modern style, but the Jan Breydel bar has old-world charm.

The Pand Hotel

MAP L4 ▪ Pandreitje 16 ▪ 05 034 06 66 ▪ www.pandhotel.com ▪ €€

This boutique hotel, in a fine 18th-century town house, is the ideal place for a romantic getaway. Close to the Burg in a pretty tree-lined street, it is beautifully decorated in a deeply upholstered style, with canopied beds.

Bonifacius

MAP K5 ▪ Groeninge 4 ▪ 05 049 00 49 ▪ www.bonifacius.be ▪ €€€

A superb boutique B&B in a 16th-century building overlooking the canal and Bonifacius Bridge. Each room is decorated with rich fabrics and antiques, and features an en suite granite bathroom with Jacuzzi bath. Bonifacius is located opposite the Michelin-starred Den Gouden Harynck restaurant (see p98).

De Tuilerieën

MAP L4 ▪ Dijver 7 ▪ 05 034 36 91 ▪ www.hotel tuilerieen.com ▪ €€€

In a 15th-century nobleman's house overlooking the canal, this lavish hotel has hosted many a celebrity. Chocolate fountain in the breakfast bar plus swimming pool, steam room and bar.

For a key to hotel price categories see p124

Bruges Hotels: Mid-range

Hotel Malleberg
MAP L4 ▪ Hoogstraat 7 ▪ 05 034 41 11 ▪ www.malleberg.be ▪ €
Located in a town house close to the Markt, this family-run establishment is a home-away-from-home. It is a tastefully decorated hotel and serves a hearty buffet breakfast in a vaulted-ceiling basement. There is free Wi-Fi available in both the guest rooms and common areas. Room rates inclusive of tickets to various attractions can be arranged.

Adornes
MAP L3 ▪ Sint-Annarei 26 ▪ 05 034 13 36 ▪ www.adornes.be ▪ Closed Jan ▪ €€
The Adornes is located in a renovated set of 16th- to 18th-century mansions overlooking the canal in the quieter, eastern part of the city, yet within walking distance of the centre. The decor, with its exposed beams, has rustic charm. Guests have free use of bicycles. Small pets are allowed. Free parking is also available.

Le Bois de Bruges
MAP J5 ▪ Vrijdagmarkt 5 ▪ 05 033 33 64 ▪ www.leboisdebruges.be ▪ €€
The Bois de Bruges is well run, with a charming plant-filled breakfast/lunch room and functional guest rooms. It overlooks the Zand, the large market square to the west of the city, and is only 10 minutes' walk from the city centre. There is a spacious car park under the hotel.

Bourgoensch Hof
MAP L4 ▪ Wollestraat 35 ▪ 05 033 16 45 ▪ www.hotelbh.be ▪ €€
Housed in a 16th-century former brewery, the Bourgoensch Hof offers good-value rooms with fabulous canal-side views. It is located in the historic centre of Bruges in a rare secluded spot.

Hotel Jacobs
MAP L2 ▪ Baliestraat 1 ▪ 05 033 98 31 ▪ www.hoteljacobs.be ▪ €€
This good-value hotel is in the peaceful Sint-Gillis neighbourhood. Housed in a traditional step-gabled building, it offers clean, comfortable public areas and cosy bedrooms with free Wi-Fi. Close to the main shops, restaurants and museums.

Jan Brito
MAP L4 ▪ Freren Fonteinstraat 1 ▪ 05 033 06 01 ▪ www.janbrito.com ▪ €€
Centrally located, between the Burg and the Koningin Astridpark, the Jan Brito is housed in a 16th-century building with a step-gabled, brick façade. The charming public rooms are decorated in Louis XVI style. There is also a pretty garden.

De' Medici
MAP L2 ▪ Potterierei 15 ▪ 050 33 98 33 ▪ www.hoteldemedici.com ▪ €€
This smart, modern hotel, overlooking the canal, is a member of the Golden Tulip group. It has a health centre with a gym, sauna and steam room, and a bar that looks over a lovely Japanese-inspired garden.

Navarra
MAP K3 ▪ Sint-Jakobsstraat 41 ▪ 05 034 05 61 ▪ www.hotelnavarra.com ▪ €€
The former trading house of the merchants of Navarre is now an elegant hotel sited to the north of the Markt. Navarra offers a high standard of service and comfort, including a fitness centre, swimming pool and jazz bar.

Oud Huis de Peellaert
MAP L4 ▪ Hoogstraat 20 ▪ 05 033 78 89 ▪ www.thepeellaert.com ▪ €€
Chandeliers, antique furniture and a beautiful spiral staircase set the tone in this pair of grand 19th-century mansions, elegantly and sympathetically restored. High standards of comfort and service prevail, with a gym and sauna in the 16th-century cellars, making this adult-only hotel a special place to stay in the heart of historic Bruges.

Prinsenhof
MAP K4 ▪ Ontvangersstraat 9 ▪ 05 034 26 90 ▪ www.prinsenhof.be ▪ €€
This regular award-winner is tucked away down a side street in the west of the city, in an area once occupied by the splendid palace of the dukes of Burgundy. Something of the dukes' grand style pervades the decor – on a smaller scale, of course. All of the comfortable guest rooms are individually decorated.

Bruges Hotels: Budget

Bauhaus Hotel
MAP M3 ■ Langestraat 33–37 ■ 05 034 10 93 ■ www.bauhaus.be ■ €
A popular, energetic and friendly hostel. Located in the east of the city, a 15-minute walk from the centre, it prides itself on its cheap accommodation. The Bauhaus bar serves more than 50 Belgian beers, and bar snacks. Free Wi-Fi.

Charlie Rockets
MAP L4 ■ Hoogstraat 19 ■ 05 033 06 60 ■ www. charlierockets.com ■ €
Located just a two-minute walk from the Burg is this party hostel, above an American-style bar with pool tables and live music on Friday nights. Free internet access. With no curfew in place, don't expect peace and quiet.

Hotel Flanders
MAP L4 ■ Langestraat 38 ■ 050 33 88 89 ■ www. hotelflanders.com ■ €
Given its central location and amenities, this modern hotel is surprisingly good value for money. It features sleek and minimalist rooms, with a handful of family rooms available, too. Amenities include a small indoor swimming pool, two leafy gardens and a car park. Make the most of the hearty breakfast buffet.

Hostel de Passage
MAP K4 ■ Dweerstraat 26 ■ 05 034 02 32 ■ www. passagebruges.com ■ €
An interesting budget hotel with just 10 simple, well-presented rooms (six doubles, two triples and two quadruples; prices quoted are per person). It is attached to the equally alluring Gran Kaffee de Passage (see p99).

Hotel Canalview Ter Reien
MAP L3 ■ Langestraat 1 ■ 05 034 91 00 ■ www. canalviewhotel.be ■ €
Fetchingly perched beside the canal a little to the east of the Burg. Ter Reien's rooms are clean, and the double bedrooms have capsule bathrooms. A room with a courtyard view is also good. Free Wi-Fi.

Lucca
MAP K3 ■ Naaldenstraat 30 ■ 05 034 20 67 ■ www.hotellucca.be ■ €
The 18th-century Neo-Classical exterior conceals an even older interior, with a vaulted medieval cellar in which guests breakfast. This was once the lodge of the merchants of Lucca – with connections to Giovanni Arnolfini, the banker who features in Jan van Eyck's famous painting, *The Arnolfini Portrait*. The rooms are quaintly old-fashioned – a fact reflected in the attractive room price.

De Pauw
MAP L2 ■ Sint-Gilliskerkhof 8 ■ 05 033 71 18 ■ www.hotelde pauw.be ■ €
This pretty, family-run hotel, with its weathered brick exterior draped with flowers, is located close to the old parish church of Sint-Gillis, in the quiet and historic northern part of town – but still just a 10-minute walk from the centre. The interior is styled like a private home, with a welcome to match.

Hotel Ter Brughe
MAP K3 ■ Oost Gistelhof 2 ■ 05 034 03 24 ■ www. hotelterbrughe.com ■ €€
Hotel Ter Brughe is located just north of the Augustijnenrei canal in a charming web of old streets. This well-run hotel occupies a listed 16th-century house overlooking the canal, which features some impressive ancient wooden beams, especially in the breakfast room and in some of the spacious guest rooms.

Patritius
MAP L3 ■ Riddersstraat 11 ■ 05 033 84 54 ■ www. hotelpatritius.be ■ €€
Given its reasonable prices, the family-owned Patritius occupies a surprisingly grand 19th-century mansion located to the north-east of the Markt. The stylish rooms and interior garden are bonuses too.

Ter Duinen
MAP L2 ■ Langerei 52 ■ 05 033 04 37 ■ www. terduinen.eu ■ €€
This charming small hotel may seem a little out of the way in the north of the city, but the centre of Bruges is only a 15-minute walk away. Well-presented rooms (some with canal views) are double-glazed and air-conditioned, and the public rooms are stylish.

For a key to hotel price categories see p124

Antwerp Hotels

Pulcinella Hostel
MAP T2 ▪ Bogaardeplein
1 ▪ 03 234 03 14 ▪ www.
jeugdherbergen.be ▪ €
This is possibly the
smartest youth hostel in
Belgium. It has a minimalist interior with a mix of
two-, four- and six-bed
rooms. There's also a bar.
Accessible for differently
abled travellers.

Quality Hotel
Antwerpen
Centrum Opera
MAP U2
▪ Molenbergstraat 9–11
▪ 03 232 76 75 ▪ www.
qualityhotel-antwerp.com
▪ €
Located just behind the
Meir shopping street,
this chain hotel is fresh,
modern and efficient.
Rooms are spacious and
comfortable. There is a
delicious breakfast buffet
and a cosy bar with a
good choice of wines.

Firean
Karel Oomsstraat 6 ▪ 03
237 02 60 ▪ www.firean.
hotelantwerpen.net ▪ €€
A highly respected family-
run hotel in a 1920s Art
Deco mansion. Although
located further out of the
centre than other options,
Firean's charm makes
the journey worthwhile.
Rooms are spacious and
feature rich fabrics.

Hotel Docklands
Kempisch Dok Westkaai
84–90 ▪ 03 231 07 26
▪ www.hoteldocklands.be
▪ €€
Situated in the up-and-
coming docklands a
15-minute walk north of
the centre, this Best
Western-owned hotel has
smartly designed colour
schemes in the rooms
and public areas. There is
a well-stocked breakfast
buffet and plenty of dining
options nearby.

Hotel Rubens
MAP T1 ▪ Oude Beurs 29
▪ 03 222 48 48 ▪ www.
hotelrubensantwerp.be
▪ €€
A quiet, romantic option
located just behind the
Grote Markt. Spacious
one-bedroom suites have
separate living rooms and
lovely views. In summers,
opt to sit outdoors on the
terrace for breakfast.

Julien
MAP T1 ▪ Korte
Nieuwstraat 24 ▪ 03 229
06 00 ▪ www.hotel-julien.
com ▪ €€
Fashioned out of two town
houses linked by a green
patio, this contemporary
hotel has stylish interiors.
Ideally located between
the Meir shopping area
and the cathedral.

Matelote
MAP T2 ▪ Haarstraat 11A
▪ 03 201 88 00 ▪ www.
hotel-matelote.be ▪ €€
Set in a converted town
house near the River
Scheldt, this hotel offers
nine dazzlingly light
rooms, all with minimal-
ist decor and modern
facilities. Prices include
Wi-Fi and mineral water;
a buffet breakfast is available at an additional cost.

Mercure Antwerp
City Centre
MAP V3 ▪ Quinten
Matsijslei 25 ▪ 03 231
15 15 ▪ www.accorhotels.
com ▪ €€
This unassuming modern
hotel is part of the small
Leopold group. The hotel
is well run, agreeably
comfortable and con-
veniently located within
easy walking distance of
Centraal station, the
Rubenshuis and the Meir
shopping street. It has its
own bar and a gym, and
just across the street is
the pretty Stadspark.

Radisson Blu
Astrid Hotel
MAP V2 ▪ Koningin
Astridplein 7 ▪ 03 203
12 34 ▪ www.radisson
blu.com ▪ €€
Close to Centraal station,
east of the city centre, this
is a large and well-run
hotel. It offers extensive
conference facilities,
and is well suited to the
business traveller. There's
also a fitness suite and
swimming pool.

't Sandt
MAP T2 ▪ Zand 17
▪ 03 232 93 90 ▪ www.
hotel-sandt.be ▪ €€
Housed in an old patrician
mansion, this hotel is
situated to the west of the
cathedral, and is close to
the river. It has been
transformed from its
elegant "Neo-Rococo"
style into a modern luxury
hotel. All the suites,
including the luxurious
penthouse, are set around
a courtyard garden.

Theater Hotel
MAP U2 ▪ Arenbergstraat
30 ▪ 03 203 54 10 ▪ www.
theater-hotel.be ▪ €€
In the theatre district
of Antwerp, this modern
hotel lies in a convenient
location close to the
Rubenshuis, and is
a short walk from the
cathedral via some of
Antwerp's best shopping
streets. The rooms are
decorated in a neat
minimalist style.

Ghent Hotels

Hostel Uppelink
MAP P2 ▪ Sint-Michielsplein 21 ▪ 09 279 44 77 ▪ www.hostel uppelink.com ▪ €
A family-owned youth hostel in a historic building beside the Sint-Michielsbrug at the heart of Ghent. Bedrooms and bathrooms are shared between two to 10 people, and there is a buffet breakfast and a small bar stocked with reasonably priced Belgian beers. The hostel also has kayaks available for renting and offers free walking tours.

Hotel Onderbergen
MAP P3 ▪ Onderbergen 69 ▪ 09 223 62 00 ▪ www.hotelonderbergen.be ▪ €
Just 3 minutes' walk from Sint-Baafskathedraal, this boutique hotel is decorated in a cool, pared-down style, Hotel Onderbergen occupies a historical house, where some of the rooms have exposed beams, and also offers family rooms for up to six people, and an apartment.

Monasterium PoortAckere
MAP P2 ▪ Oude Houtlei 56 ▪ 09 269 22 10 ▪ www.monasterium.be ▪ €
Here is an interesting experience: a hotel in a converted convent. An air of tranquillity pervades the (largely 19th-century) buildings and grounds. A special place, enhanced by a warm welcome and a relaxed atmosphere – and a convenient location just west of the city centre.

Erasmus Hotel
MAP P2 ▪ Poel 25 ▪ 09 224 21 95 ▪ www.erasmushotel.be ▪ €€
This 16th-century patrician's house, west of the city centre, retains many of its original features and is decorated with antiques. Its old-fashioned charm creates the perfect backdrop for visiting the historic city.

Ghent River Hotel
MAP Q1 ▪ Waaistraat 5 ▪ 09 266 10 10 ▪ www.ghent-river-hotel.be ▪ €€
This functional, modern hotel has 77 rooms occupying a converted 16th-century house and a 19th-century factory. It is located on the bank of the River Leie close to the lively Vrijdagmarkt. The breakfast room offers stunning views of the city.

Hotel de Flandre
MAP P2 ▪ Poel 1–2 ▪ 09 266 06 00 ▪ www.hotel deflandre.be ▪ €€
Tucked behind the Korenlei quayside, this stylish townhouse has retained plenty of period detail in its public areas while its bedrooms are calm and comfortable.

Hotel Gravensteen
MAP P1 ▪ Jan Breydelstraat 35 ▪ 09 225 11 50 ▪ www.gravensteen.be ▪ €€
Sitting opposite the Castle of the Counts, this hotel has a wow-factor entrance, comfortable rooms, a cosy bar, sauna and fitness room. The breakfast buffet offers a great selection of hot and cold choices. Guests have access to a private car park and are permitted to bring small pets.

Hotel Harmony
MAP Q1 ▪ Kraanlei 37 ▪ 09 324 26 80 ▪ www.hotel-harmony.be ▪ €€
A stylish, family-run hotel located in Patershol, the oldest quarter of Ghent. The hotel features a heated courtyard swimming pool and a series of upscale rooms facing the canal; all have roof terraces with views over the city.

Ibis Gent Centrum Kathedraal
MAP Q2 ▪ Limburgstraat 2 ▪ 09 233 00 00 ▪ www.accorhotels.com ▪ €€
Right in the centre of Ghent, overlooking Sint-Baafskathedraal, this is a well-run, modern and attractive member of the reliable Ibis chain. There are plenty of restaurants to choose from nearby. The private paying car park has limited spaces.

NH Gent Belfort
MAP Q2 ▪ Hoogpoort 63 ▪ 09 233 33 31 ▪ www.nh-hotels.com ▪ €€
This chain certainly knows how to deliver style and comfort. The Belfort has all the facilities of a hotel of this rank, including a fitness room and sauna, and is centrally located, opposite the Stadhuis.

Pillows Grand Hotel Reylof
MAP P2 ▪ Hoogstraat 36 ▪ 09 235 40 70 ▪ www.pillowshotels.com ▪ €€
A grand 18th-century mansion and a modern extension provide luxury accommodation close to the historic centre. There is a courtyard garden, bar, highly regarded restaurant, and a "wellness centre".

For a key to hotel price categories see p124

General Index

Acknowledgments

This edition updated by

Contributor Teresa Fisher
Senior Editor Alison McGill
Project Editors Parnika Bagla, Elspeth Beidas
Project Art Editor Ankita Sharma
Editors Chhavi Nagpal, Anuroop Sanwalia
Picture Research Administrator
Vagisha Pushp
Picture Research Manager Taiyaba Khatoon
Publishing Assistant Halima Mohammed
Jacket Designer Jordan Lambley
Cartographer Ashif
Cartography Manager Suresh Kumar
Senior Production Editor Jason Little
Senior Production Controller Samantha Cross
Deputy Managing Editor Beverly Smart
Managing Editors Shikha Kulkarni,
Hollie Teague
Managing Art Editor Sarah Snelling
Senior Managing Art Editor Priyanka Thakur
Art Director Maxine Pedliham
Publishing Director Georgina Dee

DK would like to thank the following for
their contribution to the previous editions:
Hilary Bird, Antony Mason

Museum of Natural Sciences, Brussels:
Th. Hubin 86tr.

Patrick Devos: 98bl.

Rex by Shutterstock: 4cra, 28clb, Colorsport 43clb.

Robert Harding Picture Library: Tibor Bognar 13br; Heinz-Dieter Falkenstein 47cl; Marc De Ganck 57br; Gunter Kirsch 29tl; Martin Moxter 7tl; Peter Richardson 8tl; Phil Robinson 103cl; Riccardo Sala 109c.

Royal Museum of Fine Arts of Belgium, Brussels: © DACS 2016 18–9; Johan Geleyns 18cl, 18b, 19cb, 73clb, 85cl.

Photo Scala, Florence: Bl, ADAGP, Paris /© DACS 2016 19tl.

Stad Antwerpen: MAS/Filip Dujardin 49tr; Museum Ann de Stroom/Hugo Maertens 50crb; Museum Ann de Stroom 100tl; Museum Mayer van den Bergh 102br; Rubenshuis 36tr, 36cl, 36–7, 101crb, /Bart Huysmans 37crb, /Michel Wuyts 36br; Michel Wuyts 104tl.

STAM: 110br.

SuperStock: age fotostock/Sara Janini 9cr; Christie's Images Ltd 45br; Fine Art Images 31cl; Iberfoto 13c, 32, 33tl, 33cl, 33bl.

La Taverne du Passage: Dominique Rodenbach 81cr.

Van Buuren Museum: 83crb.

Cover

Front and spine: **Alamy Stock Photo:** John Kellerman.

Back: **Alamy Stock Photo:** Nattee Chalermtiragool tr, John Kellerman b; Jochen Tack crb; **Dreamstime.com:** Emicristea cl, Aleksandra Lande tl.

Pull Out Map Cover

Alamy Stock Photo: John Kellerman.

All other images © Dorling Kindersley
For further information see:
www.dkimages.com

Illustrator: chrisorr.com.

Penguin
Random
House

First edition 2004

Published in Great Britain by
Dorling Kindersley Limited
DK, One Embassy Gardens, 8 Viaduct
Gardens, London SW11 7BW, UK

The authorised representative in the EEA is
Dorling Kindersley Verlag GmbH. Arnulfstr.
124, 80636 Munich, Germany

Published in the United States by
DK Publishing, 1745 Broadway, 20th Floor,
New York, NY 10019, USA

Copyright © 2004, 2022 Dorling
Kindersley Limited
A Penguin Random House Company

22 23 24 25 10 9 8 7 6 5 4 3 2 1

A CIP catalogue record is available
from the British Library.

A catalogue record for this book is available
from the Library of Congress.

ISSN 1479-344X

ISBN 978-0-2414-6280-5

Printed and bound in China

www.dk.com

*As a guide to abbreviations in visitor information blocks: **Adm** = admission charge; **D** = dinner.*

MIX
Paper from
responsible sources

FSC™ C018179

This book was made with Forest
Stewardship Council™ certified
paper – one small step in DK's
commitment to a sustainable future.
For more information go to
www.dk.com/our-green-pledge

Phrase Book: French

In an Emergency

Help!	**Au secours!**	*oh sekoor*
Stop!	**Arrêtez!**	*aret-ay*
Call a doctor	**Appelez un medecin**	*apuh-lay uñ medsañ*
Call the police	**Appelez la police**	*apuh-lay lah pol-ees*
Call the fire brigade	**Appelez les pompiers**	*apuh-lay leh poñ-peeyay*
Where is the nearest telephone?	**Où est le téléphone le plus proche**	*oo ay luh tehlehfon luh ploo prosh*

Communication Essentials

Yes/No	**Oui/Non**	*wee/noñ*
Please	**S'il vous plaît**	*seel voo play*
Thank you	**Merci**	*mer-see*
Excuse me	**Excusez-moi**	*exkoo-zay mwah*
Hello	**Bonjour**	*boñzhoor*
Goodbye	**Au revoir**	*oh ruh-vwar*
Good evening	**Bon soir**	*boñ-swar*
morning	**Le matin**	*matañ*
afternoon	**L'apres-midi**	*l'apreh-meedee*
evening	**Le soir**	*swah*
yesterday	**Hier**	*eeyehr*
today	**Aujourd'hui**	*oh-zhoor-dwee*
tomorrow	**Demain**	*duhmañ*
here	**Ici**	*ee-see*
there	**Là bas**	*lah bah*
What?	**Quel/quelle?**	*kel, kel*
When?	**Quand?**	*koñ*
Why?	**Pourquoi?**	*poor-kwah*
Where?	**Où?**	*oo*

Useful Phrases

How do you do?	**Comment allez vous?**	*kom-moñ talay voo*
Very well, thank you	**Très bien, merci**	*treh byañ, mer-see*
How are you?	**Comment ça va?**	*kom-moñ sah vah*
See you soon	**À bientôt**	*ah byañ-toh*
That's fine	**Ça va bien**	*sah vah byañ*
Where is/are …?	**Où est/sont …?**	*ooh ay/soñ*
Which way to …?	**Quelle est la direction pour …?**	*kel ay lah deer-ek-syoñ poor*
Do you speak English?	**Parlez-vous anglais?**	*par-lay voo oñg-lay?*
I don't understand	**Je ne comprends pas**	*zhuh nuh kom-proñ pah*
I'm sorry	**Excusez-moi**	*exkoo-zay mwah*

Shopping

How much?	**C'est combien?**	*say kom-byañ*
I would like …	**Je voudrais**	*zhuh voo-dray*
Do you have …?	**Est-ce que vous avez …?**	*es-kuh voo zavay*
Do you take credit cards?	**Est-ce que vous acceptez les cartes de crédit?**	*es-kuh voo zaksept-ay leh kart duh kreh-dee*
What time do you open/ close?	**À quelle heure vous êtes ouvert/ fermé?**	*ah kel urr voo zet oo-ver/ fermay*
this one	**celui-ci**	*suhl-wee see*
that one	**celui-là**	*suhl-wee lah*
expensive	**cher**	*shehr*
cheap	**pas cher, bon marché**	*pah shehr, boñ mar-shay*

size (clothing)	**la taille**	*tye*
white	**blanc**	*bloñ*
black	**noir**	*nwahr*
red	**rouge**	*roozh*
yellow	**jaune**	*zhownh*
green	**vert**	*vehr*
blue	**bleu**	*bluh*

Types of Shop

bakery	**la boulangerie**	*booloñ-zhuree*
bank	**la banque**	*boñk*
bookshop	**la librairie**	*lee-brehree*
butcher	**la boucherie**	*boo-shehree*
cake shop	**la pâtisserie**	*patee-sree*
chemist	**la pharmacie**	*farmah-see*
chip shop/stand	**la friterie**	*free-tuh-ree*
chocolate shop	**le chocolatier**	*shok-oh-lah-tyeh*
delicatessen	**la charcuterie**	*shah-koo-tuh-ree*
department store	**le grand magasin**	*groñ maga-zañ*
fishmonger	**la poissonerie**	*pwasson-ree*
greengrocer	**le marchand de légumes**	*mar-shoñ duh lay-goom*
hairdresser	**le coiffeur**	*kwafuhr*
market	**le marché**	*marsh ay*
newsagent	**le magasin de journaux/tabac**	*maga-zañ duh zhoor-no/ta-bak*
post office	**le bureau de poste**	*boo-roh duh pohst*
shop	**le magasin**	*maga-zañ*
supermarket	**le supermarché**	*soo-pehr-marshay*
travel agency	**l'agence de voyage**	*azhons duh vwayazh*

Sightseeing

art gallery	**la galérie d'art**	*galer-ree dart*
bus station	**la gare routière**	*gahr roo-tee-yehr*
cathedral	**la cathédrale**	*katay-dral*
church	**l'église**	*aygleez*
closed on public holiday	**fermeture jour ferié**	*fehrmeh-tur zhoor fehree-ay*
garden	**le jardin**	*zhah-dañ*
library	**la bibliothèque**	*beebleeo-tek*
museum	**le musée**	*moo-zay*
railway station	**la gare (SNCB)**	*gahr (es-en-say-bay)*
tourist office	**les informations**	*uñ-for-mah-syoñ*
town hall	**l'hôtel de ville**	*ohtel duh vil*
train	**le train**	*trañ*

Staying in a Hotel

Do you have a vacant room?	**est-ce que vous avez une chambre?**	*es-kuh voo zavay oon shambr*
double room	**la chambre à deux personnes**	*shambr ah duh per-son*
with double bed	**avec un grand lit**	*ah-vek uñ groñ lee*
twin room	**la chambre à deux lits**	*shambr ah duhlee*
single room	**la chambre à une personne**	*shambr ah oon pehr-son*
room with a bath shower	**la chambre avec salle de bain une douche**	*shambr ah-vek sal duh bañ doosh*
I have a reservation	**J'ai fait une reservation**	*zhay fay oon ray-zehrva-syoñ*

Eating Out

Have you got a table?	**Avez vous une table libre?**	*avay-voo oon tahbl leebr*
I would like to reserve	**Je voudrais réserver**	*zhuh voo-dray rayzehr-vay*
a table	**une table**	*oon tahbl*
The bill, please	**L'addition, s'il vous plait**	*l'adee-syoñ, seel voo play*
I am a vegetarian	**Je suis végétarien**	*zhuh swee vezhay-tehryañ*
waiter/ waitress	**Monsieur/ Mademoiselle**	*muh-syur/ mad-uh-mwah-zel*
menu	**le menu**	*men-oo*
wine list	**la carte des vins**	*lah kart-deh vañ*
glass	**verre**	*vehr*
bottle	**la bouteille**	*boo-tay*
knife	**le couteau**	*koo-toh*
fork	**la fourchette**	*for-shet*
spoon	**la cuillère**	*kwee-yehr*
breakfast	**le petit déjeuner**	*puh-tee day-zhuh-nay*
lunch	**le déjeuner**	*day-zhuh-nay*
dinner	**le dîner**	*dee-nay*
main course	**le grand plat**	*groñ plah*
starter	**l'hors d'oeuvre**	*or duhvr*
dessert	**le dessert**	*deh-zehrt*
dish of the day	**le plat du jour**	*plah doo joor*
bar	**le bar**	*bah*
café	**le café**	*ka-fay*
rare	**saignant**	*say-nyoñ*
medium	**à point**	*ah pwañ*
well done	**bien cuit**	*byañ kwee*

Menu Decoder

agneau	*ahnyoh*	lamb
ail	*eye*	garlic
asperges	*ahs-pehrj*	asparagus
bar/loup	*bah/loo*	bass
de mer	*duh mare*	
bière	*byahr*	beer
boeuf	*buhf*	beef
brochet	*brosh-ay*	pike
café	*kah-fay*	coffee
café au lait	*kah-fay oh lay*	white coffee
caffe latte	*kah-fay lat-uh*	milky coffee
canard	*kanar*	duck
cerf/chevreuil	*surf/shev-roy*	venison
chicon	*shee-koñ*	Belgian endive
chocolat chaud	*shok-oh-lah shoh*	hot chocolate
choux de Bruxelles	*shoo duh broocksell*	Brussels sprouts
coquille Saint-Jacques	*kok-eel sañ jak*	scallop
crêpe	*crayp*	pancake
crevette	*kreh-vet*	prawn
dorade	*doh-rad*	sea bream
eau	*oh*	water
epinard	*aypeenar*	spinach
faisant	*feh-zoñ*	pheasant
frites	*freet*	chips/fries
fruits	*frwee*	fruit
gauffre	*gohfr*	waffle
hareng	*ah-roñ*	herring
haricots	*arrykoh*	haricot beans
haricots verts	*arrykoh vehr*	green beans
homard	*oh-ma*	lobster
huitre	*weetr*	oyster
jus d'orange	*zhoo doh-ronj*	orange juice
légumes	*lay-goom*	vegetables
limonade	*lee-moh-nad*	lemonade
lotte	*lot*	monkfish
moule	*mool*	mussel

poisson	*pwah-ssoñ*	fish
pommes de terre	*pom-duh tehr*	potatoes
porc	*por*	pork
poulet	*poo-lay*	chicken
raie	*ray*	skate
saumon	*soh-moñ*	salmon
thé	*tay*	tea
thon	*toñ*	tuna
truffe	*troof*	truffle
truite	*trweet*	trout
veau	*voh*	veal
viande	*vee-yand*	meat
vin	*vañ*	wine
vin maison	*vañ may-sañ*	house wine

Numbers

0	**zéro**	*zeh-roh*
1	**un, une**	*uñ, oon*
2	**deux**	*duh*
3	**trois**	*trwah*
4	**quatre**	*katr*
5	**cinq**	*sañk*
6	**six**	*sees*
7	**sept**	*set*
8	**huit**	*weet*
9	**neuf**	*nurf*
10	**dix**	*dees*
11	**onze**	*oñz*
12	**douze**	*dooz*
13	**treize**	*trehz*
14	**quatorze**	*katorz*
15	**quinze**	*kañz*
16	**seize**	*sehz*
17	**dix-sept**	*dees-set*
18	**dix-huit**	*dees-zweet*
19	**dix-neuf**	*dees-znurf*
20	**vingt**	*vañ*
21	**vingt-et-un**	*vañ ay uhn*
30	**trente**	*tront*
40	**quarante**	*karoñt*
50	**cinquante**	*sañkoñt*
60	**soixante**	*swahsoñt*
70	**septante**	*setoñt*
80	**quatre-vingt**	*katr-vañ*
90	**quatre-vingt-dix/ nonante**	*katr vañ dees/ nonañ*
100	**cent**	*soñ*
1000	**mille**	*meel*
1,000,000	**million**	*miyoñ*

Time

What is the time?	**Quelle heure est-il?**	*kel uhr eh-til*
one minute	**une minute**	*oon mee-noot*
one hour	**une heure**	*oon uhr*
half an hour	**une demi-heure**	*oon duh-mee uhr*
half past one	**une heure et demi**	*oon uhr ay duh-mee*
a day	**un jour**	*zhuhr*
a week	**une semaine**	*suh-men*
a month	**un mois**	*mwah*
a year	**une année**	*annay*
Monday	**lundi**	*luñ-dee*
Tuesday	**mardi**	*mahr-dee*
Wednesday	**mercredi**	*mehrkruh-dee*
Thursday	**jeudi**	*zhuh-dee*
Friday	**vendredi**	*voñdruh-dee*
Saturday	**samedi**	*sam-dee*
Sunday	**dimanche**	*dee-moñsh*

Phrase Book: Dutch

In an Emergency

Help!	**Help!**	*help*
Stop!	**Stop!**	*stop*
Call a doctor!	**Haal een dokter!**	*haal uhndok-tur*
Call the police!	**Roep de politie!**	*roop duh poe-leet-see*
Call the fire brigade!	**Roep de brandweer!**	*roop duh brahnt-vheer*
Where is the nearest telephone?	**Waar ist de dichtsbijzijnde telefoon?**	*vhaar iss duh dikst-baiy-zaiyn duh tay-luh-foan*
Where is the nearest hospital?	**Waar ist het dichtsbijzijnde ziekenhuis?**	*vhaar iss het dikst-baiy-zaiyn -duh zee-kuh-hows*

Communication Essentials

Yes	**Ja**	*yaa*
No	**Nee**	*nay*
Please	**Alstublieft**	*ahls-tew-bleeft*
Thank you	**Dank u**	*dhank-ew*
Excuse me	**Pardon**	*pahr-don*
Hello	**Hallo**	*haa-lo*
Goodbye	**Dag**	*dahgh*
Good night	**Goedenacht**	*ghoot-e-naakt*
morning	**Morgen**	*mor-ghugh*
afternoon	**Middag**	*mid-dahgh*
evening	**Avond**	*av-vohnd*
yesterday	**Gisteren**	*ghis-tern*
today	**Vandaag**	*van-daagh*
tomorrow	**Morgen**	*mor-ghugh*
here	**Hier**	*heer*
there	**Daar**	*daar*
What?	**Wat?**	*vhat*
When?	**Wanneer?**	*vhan-eer*
Why?	**Waarom?**	*vhaar-om*
Where?	**Waar?**	*vhaar*
How?	**Hoe?**	*hoo*

Useful Phrases

How are you?	**Hoe gaat het ermee?**	*hoo ghaat het er-may*
Very well, thank you	**Heel goed, dank u**	*hayl ghoot, dhank ew*
How do you do?	**Hoe maakt u het?**	*hoo maakt ew het*
See you soon	**Tot ziens**	*tot zeens*
That's fine	**Prima**	*pree-mah*
Where is/are …?	**Waar is/zijn …?**	*vhaar iss/zayn*
How far is it to …?	**Hoe ver is het naar …?**	*hoo vehr iss het nar*
How do I get to …?	**Hoe kom ik naar …?**	*hoo kom ik nar*
Do you speak English?	**Spreekt u engels?**	*spraykt uw eng-uhls*
I don't understand	**Ik snap het niet**	*ik snahp het neet*
Could you speak slowly?	**Kunt u langzamer praten?**	*kuhnt ew lahng-zarmer-praat-tuh*
I'm sorry	**Sorry**	*sorry*

Shopping

I'm just looking	**Ik kijk alleen even**	*ik kaiyk alleyn ay-vuh*
How much does this cost?	**Hoeveel kost dit?**	*hoo-vayl kost dit*
What time do you open?	**Hoe laat gaat u open?**	*hoo laat ghaat ew opuh*
What time do you close?	**Hoe laat gaat u dicht?**	*hoo laat ghaat ew dikht*

I would like …	**Ik wil graag …**	*ik vhil ghraakh*
Do you have …?	**Heeft u …?**	*hayft ew*
Do you take credit cards?	**Neemt u credit cards aan?**	*naymt ew credit cards aan?*
Do you take travellers' cheques?	**Neemt u reischeques aan?**	*naymt ew raiys-sheks aan*
This one	**Deze**	*day-zuh*
That one	**Die**	*dee*
expensive	**duur**	*dewr*
cheap	**goedkoop**	*ghoot-koap*
size	**maat**	*maat*
white	**wit**	*vhit*
black	**zwart**	*zvhahrt*
red	**rood**	*roat*
yellow	**geel**	*ghayl*
green	**groen**	*ghroon*
blue	**blauw**	*blah-ew*

Types of Shop

antiques shop	**antiekwinkel**	*ahn-teek-vhin-kul*
bakery	**bakkerij**	*bah-ker-aiy*
bank	**bank**	*bahnk*
bookshop	**boekwinkel**	*book-vhin-kul*
butcher	**slagerij**	*slaakh-er-aiy*
cake shop	**banketbakkerij**	*bahnk-et-bahk-er-aiy*
chip stop/stand	**frituur/ frietkot**	*free-to-er/ freet-cot*
chemist/ drugstore	**apotheek**	*ah-poe-taiyk*
delicatessen	**delicatessen**	*daylee-kah-tes-suh*
department store	**warenhuis**	*vhaah-uh-houws*
fishmonger	**viswinkel**	*viss-vhin-kul*
greengrocer	**groenteboer**	*ghroon-tuh-boor*
hairdresser	**kapper**	*kah-per*
market	**markt**	*mahrkt*
newsagent	**krantenwinkel**	*krahn-tuh-vhin-kul*
post office	**postkantoor**	*pohst-kahn-tor*
supermarket	**supermarkt**	*sew-per-mahrkt*
tobacconist	**sigarenwinkel**	*see-ghaa-ruh-vhin-kul*
travel agent	**reisburo**	*raiys-bew-roa*

Sightseeing

art gallery	**gallerie**	*ghaller-ee*
bus station	**busstation**	*buhs-stah-shown*
bus ticket	**kaartje**	*kaar-tyuh*
cathedral	**kathedraal**	*kah-tuh-draal*
church	**kerk**	*kehrk*
closed on public holidays	**op feestdagen gesloten**	*op fayst-daa-ghuh ghuh-slow-tuh*
day return	**dagretour**	*dahgh-ruh-tour*
garden	**tuin**	*touwn*
library	**bibliotheek**	*bee-bee-yo-tayk*
museum	**museum**	*mew-zay-um*
railway station	**station**	*stah-shown*
return ticket	**retourtje**	*ruh-tour-tyuh*
single journey	**enkeltje**	*eng-kahl-tyuh*
tourist information	**dienst voor toerisme**	*deenst vor tor-ism*
town hall	**stadhuis**	*staht-houws*
train	**trein**	*traiyn*

Staying in a Hotel

double room with double bed	**een twees persoons- kamer met een twee persoonsbed**	*uhn tvhays per-soans- ka-mer met uhn tvhay per-soans beht*
single room	**eenpersoons- kamer**	*ayn-per-soans kaa-mer*

twin room	een kamer met een lits-jumeaux	uhn kaa-mer met uhn lee-zjoo-moh
room with a bath/shower	kaamer met bad/ douche	kaa-mer met baht/doosh
Do you have a vacant room?	Zijn er nog kamers vrij?	zaiyn er nokh kaa-mers vray
I have a reservation	Ik heb gereserveerd	ik hehp ghuh-ray-sehr-veert

Eating Out

Have you got a table?	Is er een tafel vrij?	iss ehr uhn tah-fuhl vraiy
I would like to reserve a table	Ik wil een tafel reserveren	ik vhil uhn tah-fel ray sehr-veer- uh
The bill, please	De rekening, alstublieft	duh ray-kuh-ning ahls-tew-bleeft
I am a vegetarian	Ik ben vegetariër	ik ben fay-ghuh-taahr-ee-er
waitress/waiter	serveerster/ ober	sehr-veer-ster/oh-ber
menu	de kaart	duh kaahrt
wine list	de wijnkaart	duh vhaiyn-kart
glass	het glass	het ghlahss
bottle	de fles	duh fless
knife	het mes	het mess
fork	de vork	duh fork
spoon	de lepel	duh lay-pul
breakfast	het ontbijt	het ont-baiyt
lunch	de lunch	duh lernsh
dinner	het diner	het dee-nay
main course	het hoofdgerecht	het hoaft-ghuh-rekht
starter, first course	het voorgerecht	het vhor-ghuh-rekht
dessert	het nagerecht	het naa-ghuh-rekht
dish of the day	het dagschotel	het dahg-skhoa-tel
bar	het cafe	het kaa-fay
café	het eetcafe	het ayt-kaa-fay
rare	rare	"rare"
medium	medium	"medium"
well done	doorbakken	door-bah-kuh

Menu Decoder

aardappels	aard-uppuhls	potatoes
asperges	as-puhj	asparagus
bier	beeh	beer
chocola	sho-koh-laa	chocolate
eend	aynt	duck
fazant	fay-zanh	pheasant
forel	foh-ruhl	trout
frietjes	free-tyuhs	chips/fries
fruit/vruchten	vroot/vrooh-tuh	fruit
garnaal	gar-naal	prawn
groenten	ghroon-tuh	vegetables
haring	haa-ring	herring
hertenvlees	hair-ten-flayss	venison
kalfsvlees	karfs-flayss	veal
kip	kip	chicken
knoflook	knoff-loak	garlic
koffie	coffee	coffee
kreeft	krayft	lobster
lamsvlees	lahms-flayss	lamb
lotte/zeeduivel	lot/seafuhdul	monkfish
mineraalwater	meener-aahl-vhaater	mineral water
mossel	moss-uhl	mussel
oester	ouhs-tuh	oyster
pannekoek	pah-nuh-kook	pancake
princesbonen	prins-ess-buh-nun	green beans

rog	rog	skate
rundvlees	ruhnt-flayss	beef
Sint Jacoboester/ Jacobsschelp	sind-yakob-ouhs-tuh/ yakob-scuhlp	scallop
snijbonen	snee-buh-nun	string beans
snoek	snoek	pike
spinazie	spin-a-jee	spinach
spruitjes	spruhr-tyuhs	Brussels sprouts
thee	tay	tea
tonijn	tuhn-een	tuna
truffel	truh-fuhl	truffle
varkensvlees	vahr-kuhns-flayss	pork
verse jus	vehr-suh zjhew	fresh orange juice
vis	fiss	fish
vlees	flayss	meat
wafel	vaff-uhl	waffle
water	vhaa-ter	water
wijn	vhaiyn	wine
witloof	vit-lurf	Belgian endive/chicory
zalm	sahlm	salmon
zeebars	see-buhr	seabass
zeebrasem	zee-brah-sum	sea bream

Numbers

1	een	ayn
2	twee	tvhay
3	drie	dree
4	vier	feer
5	vijf	faiyf
6	zes	zess
7	zeven	zay-vuh
8	acht	ahkht
9	negen	nay-guh
10	tien	teen
11	elf	elf
12	twaalf	tvhaalf
13	dertien	dehr-teen
14	veertien	feer-teen
15	vijftien	faiyf-teen
16	zestien	zess-teen
17	zeventien	zayvuh-teen
18	achtien	ahkh-teen
19	negentien	nay-ghuh-tien
20	twintig	tvhin-tukh
21	eenentwintig	aynuh-tvhin-tukh
30	dertig	dehr-tukh
40	veertig	feer-tukh
50	vijftig	faiyf-tukh
60	zestig	zess-tukh
70	zeventig	zay-vuh-tukh
80	tachtig	tahkh-tukh
90	negentig	nayguh-tukh
100	honderd	hohn-durt
1000	duizend	douw-zuhnt
1,000,000	miljoen	mill-yoon

Time

one minute	een minuut	uhn meen-ewt
one hour	een uur	uhn ewr
half an hour	een half uur	een hahlf uhr
half past one	half twee	hahlf twee
a day	een dag	uhn dahgh
a week	een week	uhn vhayk
a month	een maand	uhn maant
a year	een jaar	uhn jaar
Monday	maandag	maan-dahgh
Tuesday	dinsdag	dins-dahgh
Wednesday	woensdag	vhoons-dahgh
Thursday	donderdag	donder-dahgh
Friday	vrijdag	vraiy-dahgh
Saturday	zaterdag	zaater-dahgh
Sunday	zondag	zon-dahgh

Dk Eyewitness Top 10
10/31/2022

Bruss